THE JESSIE WILLCOX SMITH
MOTHER GOOSE

"No, no, my melodies will never die,
while nurses sing or babies cry"

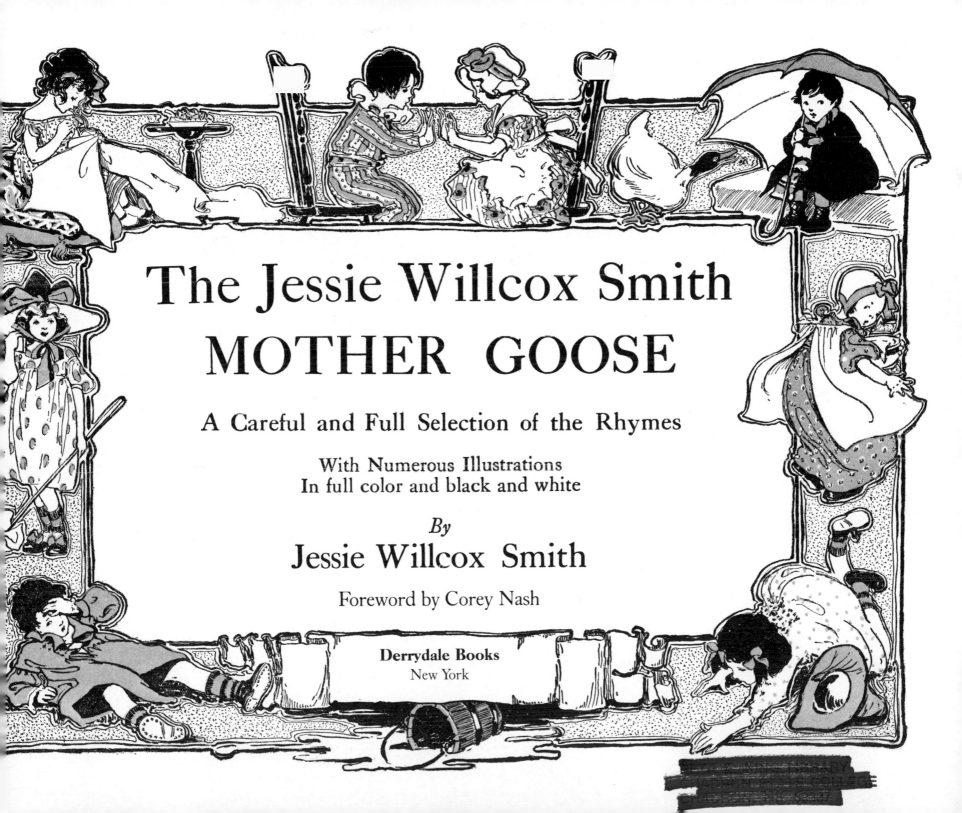

The Jessie Willcox Smith
MOTHER GOOSE

A Careful and Full Selection of the Rhymes

With Numerous Illustrations
In full color and black and white

By

Jessie Willcox Smith

Foreword by Corey Nash

Derrydale Books
New York

This 1986 edition is published by Derrydale Books, distributed by Crown Publishers, Inc.,
225 Park Avenue South, New York, New York 10003.

Printed and Bound in the United States of America

Library of Congress Cataloging-in-Publication Data
Mother Goose.
The Jessie Willcox Smith Mother Goose.

Summary: An illustrated collection of over 600 Mother Goose nursery rhymes,
including both the well-known and the less familiar rhymes.
1. Nursery rhymes   2. Children's poetry.   [1. Nursery rhymes]   I. Smith, Jessie
Willcox, 1863-1935, ill.   II. Title.
PZ8.3.M85   1986c   398'.8   86-16673
ISBN 0-517-60357-8

h g f e d c

Foreword
JESSIE WILLCOX SMITH
1863–1935

JESSIE WILLCOX SMITH was born in Philadelphia on September 6, 1863. Had she been born half a century earlier, it is very likely that we might not know her work today. For in the early nineteenth century, women artists were not given the opportunities to develop and exhibit their talents. In fact, many top art institutions did not even accept women students until later in the century. But it is not merely the fortune of her birthdate that contributed to her illustrious career as a portrayer of children.

Because of a deep love for children, Smith began her career as a kindergarten teacher and it was not until she was invited to join an art class by a female relative that she developed her artistic talents. Her early work was enthusiastically received and she was encouraged by her art teachers, family and friends to give up teaching and pursue a career as an illustrator.

In 1884, Smith enrolled in the School of Design for Women in Philadelphia for one year. She then joined the Pennsylvania Academy of the Fine Arts to study under the volatile Thomas Eakins. She flourished there for three years, at which time she left to begin her career.

Her first major illustration appeared in May 1888 in *St. Nicholas* magazine. At this time she also became a staff member of the advertising department of *The Ladies' Home Journal,* where she was a jack-of-all-trades and was also given the opportunity to develop illustrations for the magazine's advertisers.

But her inclination toward the field of fine arts soon led her to study under Howard Pyle at the Drexel Institute of Arts and Sciences, also in Philadelphia. Pyle was Smith's most inspiring teacher and one can see his influence in her work. As the founder of the Brandywine school of illustration in America, Pyle was also responsible for developing the talents of the now well-known N.C. Wyeth, Maxfield Parrish, Frank Schoonover and many others.

Besides being a master teacher and artist, Pyle was also influential in obtaining assignments for his students. Among Smith's classmates at the time were Violet Oakley and Elizabeth Shippen Green (later Elliott). Pyle was so impressed by this threesome, who became close friends for life and working partners, that he got them assignments from prestigious publishers in Philadelphia, New York and Boston.

Smith's first illustrations in book form appeared in a work of Longfellow, and she went on to illustrate close to forty other titles. Among these are works by Louisa May Alcott, Charles Dickens, Nathaniel Hawthorne and George MacDonald. Her most beloved works include *A Child's Garden of Verses* by Robert Louis Stevenson, *Little Women, The Water Babies* by Charles Kingsley, *Heidi, The Book of the Child, A Child's Book of Stories, Rhymes of Real Children, 'Twas the Night Before Christmas, At the Back of the North Wind, A Child's Prayer* and, of course, *The Jessie Willcox Smith Mother Goose.*

During the time she was working on children's books, Smith was probably best known by the public for her magazine covers and interior illustrations. Her magazine work for more than forty years included such publications as *Good Housekeeping, Collier's Weekly, House and Garden, The Ladies' Home Journal, McClure's, Century, Frank Leslie's Popular Monthly, Harper's Bazaar, Harper's Weekly, St. Nicholas, Scribner's, The Woman's Home Companion* and scores of others. Many of these illustrations were later reprinted in book form.

Her work was also awarded numerous prizes and medals and was exhibited throughout the world. In 1936, one year after Smith's death, the Pennsylvania Academy of the Fine Arts honored her in a retrospective exhibition of more than one hundred of her works.

It is ironic that Smith, a true lover of all children, never married or had her own offspring. For her work imparts the love that only a mother could know for her child. Smith wanted her children so pure and innocent that she disdained using professional models and instead preferred to search high and low for the "right" child. And we are all the more fortunate for it.

Today we see Smith's work endure on greeting cards, posters and reissued in book form. A recent addition to the book world is a beautiful new series of Children's Classics, distributed by Crown Publishers, which includes several of Smith's best works.

It is indeed a pleasure to present *The Jessie Willcox Smith Mother Goose* to you, a rare and classic edition for the entire family to enjoy. My only regret is that I could not have known Jessie Willcox Smith, as an artist and as a person.

COREY NASH

New York City
June 1986

An Historical Note

IT WAS about the year 1696 that Charles Perrault published, in France, a book entitled Mother Goose's (Mere L'Oye) Tales, which comprised Little Red Riding Hood, The Fairy (sisters of diamonds and toads), Blue Beard, Sleeping Beauty, Puss in Boots, Cinderella, Riquet with the Tuft, and Little Thum—eight in all. This is the first time that the title "Mother Goose" is known to have been used, and it is supposed that, in preparing these prose tales for publication, Perrault simply used as the title, a well-known synonym for fairy-tales.

Some years later the fame of these tales reached England, and they were there translated by one Robert Samber and published by John Newbury, of St. Paul's Churchyard, London, who was the first person to publish little books for children. Among these was a book of verse made up of old and familiar rhymes and jingles, the true origin of many of which will always be wrapped in mystery; and owing to the great success of the prose tales, he determined to call this book Mother Goose's Melodies. This volume represents the first English edition.

A controversy has existed among Mother Goose authorities concerning a report, which was first circulated about 1856, that an edition of verses entitled "Songs for the Nursery; or, Mother Goose's Melodies for Children," had been printed in Boston in 1719 by Thomas Fleet, who had married a member of the "wealthy Vergoose family," originally of Bristol, England. The story runs that one Elizabeth Goose, the mother-in-law of Fleet, sang the melodies incessently to the Fleet babies, and to the distraction of her son-in-law. She had probably been hushed to sleep in her own infancy in her English home by these same soporific sonnets. As his efforts to quiet the old lady were vain, Fleet determined to turn them to some account by publishing the book referred to.

Many years of diligent search for a copy of this edition, however, has failed to bring any to light; and the existence, therefore, of such an edition is now considered mythical. It is a significant fact in this connection that the contemporaneous writer Benjamin Franklin fails to mention such an edition anywhere among his varied writings. And we should also remember that Boston children of those days were fed mainly on Gospel food.

For the undisputed American beginning of this familiar title, we go on to the years just following our Revolutionary War, when Isaiah Thomas, the historical printer of Worcester, Massachusetts, collected stories for youngsters and copied Newbury's English issue. Two copies of the Thomas reprint are in existence, and were owned by the late Mr. W. H. Whitmore, who was probably the leading authority on Mother Goose lore in this country.

It is from a facsimile reproduction of the Thomas edition that the first fifty-one rhymes, with their morals, in the present volume are taken.   In the original edition each of the rhymes was illustrated in a most crude fashion, not by a Jessie Willcox Smith, one may be sure; the cuts being used simply because the printer had the blocks on hand.   And yet how these same primitive pictures have moulded our ideas of many of the now famous characters!

As there were only fifty-one rhymes in the original English edition, it will be readily seen that from time to time verses of the same general character have crept in, until now there are several hundred commonly known as Mother Goose's Melodies.   Many of them were refrains of popular songs, or formed parts of longer poems; some seem to be snatches of folksongs; others are corruptions of some of Shakespeare's sonnets, and Oliver Goldsmith is credited with many, for he was at that time a constant writer for Newbury's press.

In compiling the present volume a careful study has been made of all available data, as well as all previous publications of Mother Goose's rhymes of any importance; and all those of a vulgar or offensive nature have been eliminated, as well as all obviously modern ones lacking the primitive flavor—the idea being to retain, as far as possible, the traditional Mother Goose spirit throughout the volume.   As a result of this work, the present book represents a collection of over three hundred more rhymes than have appeared in any single volume previously published.

There are few children to whom the charm of Mother Goose's Melodies has not appealed; just what it is about them that has fascinated the children of so many generations is not clear to all grown-ups, but it seems to me that it is their very crudity that appeals to these little ones, who, developing as the race did, represent a more or less savage stage.   And whether the hallowed name of Mother Goose be of French, English or American origin matters little, so long as the magic of the melodies themselves continues to hold the children of the generations to come.

KATHERINE GRIDLEY BUDDY.

A List of the Rhymes

A, B, C, and D 36
A, B, C, tumble down D 130
About the bush, Willie, about the bee-hive 134
A carrion crow sat on an oak 86
A cat came fiddling out of a barn . . 98
A certain young farmer of Ayr . . 115
A curious discourse about an apple-pie 124
A diller, a dollar 150
A dog and a cat went out together. 59
A duck and a drake 65
Aena, deena, dina, duss 115
A famous old woman was Mme. McBright 88
A farmer went trotting upon his gray mare 132
A for the Ape, that we saw at the fair 93
A fox went out in a hungry plight . 111
A frog among some rushes dwelt . 131
A frog he would a-wooing go . 100, 101
A glass of milk and a slice of bread 93
A good child, a good child 142
A is Ann, with milk from the cow . 157

A jolly fat miller is Poopleton Bun 126
A little boy went into a barn 103
A little cock-sparrow sat on a green tree 38
A little cock-sparrow sat on a tree . 53
A little old man of Derby 165
A little pig found a fifty-dollar note 148
All of a row 97
*A long-tailed pig, or a short-tailed pig 20
A man of words and not of deeds. 108
A man went a-hunting at Reigate. 35
A-milking, a-milking, my maid . . . 38
An apple-pie when it looks nice . . . 161
A nick and a nock 165
An old woman lived in Nottingham town 46
An old woman was sweeping her house 120, 123
A pie sate on a pear-tree 43
Apple-pie, pudding, and pancake . . 148
Arithmetic, I studied so 133
Around the green gravel 43
A red sky, etc 43
Arthur O'Bower has broken his band 101

As I walked by myself 155
As I was going along, long, long . . 55
As I was going to market upon a market-day 44
As I was going to sell my eggs 134
As I was going up and down 33
As I was going up Pippin Hill 84
As I was going up the hill 166
As little Jenny Wren 87
As the days grow longer 115
As Tittymouse sat in the witty to spin 38
As Tommy Snooks and Bessy Brooks 34
A sunshine shower 35
A sunshiny shower 86
A swarm of bees in May 35
At early morn the spiders spin 172
At reck'ning let's play 172
At the siege of Belleisle 160
Awake, arise, pull out your eyes . . . 142
A was an angler 71, 72, 73
A was an apple-pie 40
A was an archer 136
Away, birds away! 142
A whale, I am told 70

Asterisk (*) indicates the 51 original Rhymes.

*BAA, baa, black sheep....... 20
Barber, barber, shave a pig...... 80
Barney Bodkin broke his nose.... 144
Bat, bat, come under my hat..... 143
Bell horses, bell horses, what time
   of day..................... 62
Bessy Bell and Mary Gray....... 74
Billy, Billy, come and play....... 47
Birds of a feather flock together.. 86
Bless you, bless you, bonny bee... 99
Blow, wind, blow! and go, mill, go! 97
Bobby Shaftoe's gone to sea...... 46
Bonny lass, pretty lass, wilt thou be
   mine?.................... 112
Bossy-cow, bossy-cow, where do you
   lie?...................... 42
Bow-wow, says the dog......... 84
*Bow-wow-wow 19
*Boys and girls, come out to play.. 19
Brow brinky.................. 81
Bryan O'Lin and his wife........ 34
Bryan O'Lin had no breeches to
   wear 47
Burnie bee, burnie bee.......... 63
Butterfly, butterfly, whence do you
   come? 96
Buttons a farthing a pair........ 56
Buz, quoth the blue fly......... 99
Bye, baby bumpkin............. 35
Bye, baby bunting.............. 81

CACKLE, cackle, Madam Goose 160
Cantaloupes! Cantaloupes! What
   is the price?................ 171
Charley, Charley, stole the barley. 107
Charley loves good cake and ale... 81
Charley Wag.................. 35

Charley Warley had a cow...... 40
Christmas comes but once a year.. 86
Clap hands, clap hands!........ 137
Clap, clap handies............. 78
*Cock a-doodle doo..........30-158
Cocks crow in the morn........ 105
Cold and raw the North winds
   blow 149
Come dance a jig.............. 134
Come hither, little puppy dog..... 76
Come hither, sweet robin........ 82
Come, let's to bed!............. 51
Come, my children, come away.... 50
Come, my dear children........ 78
Come, take up your hats........ 69
Come to the window........... 172
Come when you're called........ 104
"Croak!" said the toad......... 94
*Cross Patch................... 26
Cry, baby, cry................ 118
Cuckoo, cherry-tree............ 103
Curly locks! Curly locks! wilt thou
   be mine?.................. 166
Currahoo, curr dhoo........... 110
Cushy cow bonny.............. 51

DAFFY-Down-Dilly 94
Dame, get up and bake your pies.. 149
Dame Trot and her cat.......... 61
Dance a baby diddy............. 145
Dance, little baby, dance up high.. 34
Dance to your daddy........... 36
Darby and Joan were dress'd in
   black 46
Deedle, deedle, dumpling, my son
   John 56
Dickery, dickery, dare.......... 67
*Dickory, dickory, dock........ 22

Diddledy, diddledy, dumpty...... 81
Did you see my wife?.......... 50
*Ding, dong, bell...........29-171
Ding, dong, darrow............ 83
Dingty Diddledy, my mammy's
   maid 129
Doctor Faustus was a good man.. 84
Doctor Foster went to Gloster.... 138
Dogs in the garden, catch 'em,
   Towser 84
Donkey, donkey, old and gray.... 74
Doodle, doodle, doo............ 80
Draw a pail of water........... 114

EARLY to bed and early to rise. 60
Eggs, butter, cheese, bread...... 156
Elizabeth, Elspeth, Betsy and Bess. 54
Elsie Marley has grown so fine... 81
Everybody in this land.......... 129

FA, Fe, Fi, Fo, Fum!........ 60
Father, may I go to war?........ 73
Father Short came down the lane.. 97
F for Fig.................... 173
Fiddle-de-dee, fiddle-de-dee....... 56
"Fire! Fire!" said the town crier.. 82
For every evil under the sun...... 39
For want of a nail, the shoe was
   lost 97
Four and twenty tailors......... 140
Friday night's dream on Saturday
   told 68

GAY go up, and gay go down.. 173
Give my horse a ton of hay...... 156
God bless the master of this house. 82
Good people of all, of every sort.. 144

Goosey, goosey, gander 55
Georgey, porgey, pudding and pie . 66
Go to bed first, a golden purse 39
Go to bed, Tom 52
*Great A, little A, Bouncing B 25
Great A, little A 118

HANDY Spandy, Jack-a-dandy . 138
Hark! hark! the dogs do bark 39
Have you seen the old woman of
  Banbury Cross? 124
Hector Protector was dressed all in
  green 119
*Heigh, diddle, diddle 24
Heigh, ding-a-ding, what shall I
  sing? 143
Here am I, little jumping Joan . . . 90
Here comes a poor woman from
  baby-land 92
Here goes my lord 138
*Here's A, B, C, D, E, F, and G . . 19
Here's Sulky Sue 119
Here stands a post 118
Here we come gathering nuts in
  May 99
Here we go up, up, up 82
He that would thrive 133
Hey diddle, dinketty, pompetty, pet 108
Hey, dorolot, dorolot! 62
Hickory Dickory Sackory down . . . 160
Hickery Dickery 6 and 7 37
Hickety, pickety, my black hen 143
High diddle ding 85
High diddle doubt, my candle's out . 74
Hinkminx! the old witch winks . . . 74
Hiram Gordon, where's your pa? . 96
Hogs in the garden, catch 'em,
  Towser 134

Hop away, skip away, my baby
  wants to play 133
Hot cross buns 88
How many days has my baby to
  play? 137
Hub-a-dub-dub 62
Hurly, burly, trumpet trace 103
Hush-a-bye, baby, Daddy is near . . 65
*Hush-a-bye, baby, on the tree-top . 23
Hush, baby, my doll 54
Hush, thee, my babby 161

I BOUGHT a dozen new-laid
  eggs 33
I do not like thee, Dr. Fell 40
I doubt, I doubt my fire's all out . . . 103
If all the seas were one sea 37
If all the world were apple-pie 54
If all the world were water 59
If a man who turnips cries 156
If I'd as much money as I could
  spend 55
If ifs and ands 105
If I had a donkey that wouldn't go . 105
If I had a mule, Sir 148
If you are a gentleman 124
If wishes were horses, beggars
  would ride 78
I had a little boy 135
I had a little cow 123
I had a little dog 39
I had a little hen 70
I had a little hobby-horse 133
I had a little husband 54
I had a little moppet 161
I had a little nut-tree 105
I had a little pony 37
I had four brothers over the sea . . . 106
I had two pigeons bright and gay . . 105

I have been to market, my lady 144
I sing, I sing 172
I'll sing you a song 87
I'll tell you a story 115
I like little pussy, her coat is so
  warm 53
I love sixpence, pretty little sixpence 103
I love you well, my little brother . . . 83
In a cottage in Fife 83
In April's sweet month 43
In fir tar is 90
Intery, mintery, cutery, corn 137
I saw a peacock with a fiery tail . . . 129
I saw a ship a-sailing 50
I saw three ships come sailing by . . 109
*Is John Smith within? 19
It costs little Gossip her income for
  shoes 93
It's raining, it's pouring 139
I've got a rocket in my pocket 96
I will sing you a song 109
*I won't be my father's Jack 22
*I would if I cou'd 21

*JACK and Jill went up the hill . . 30
Jack, be nimble; Jack, be quick . . . 104
*Jack Spratt could eat no fat 20
Jack Spratt had a cat 138
Jack Spratt's pig 65
Jacky, come give me your fiddle . . . 159
January brings the snow 119
Jeannie, come tie my 103
Jerry Hall, he is so small 68
Jockety jog—jockety jog 169
Jockey was a piper's son 123
John, come sell thy fiddle 112
John Cook had a little gray mare . . 37
John fought for his beloved land . . 96
Johnny Armstrong kill'd a calf . . . 149

Johnny shall have a new bonnet... 110
Johnny's too little to whittle...... 135
John O'Gudgeon was a wild man.. 135
Joseph Smith bought a rake...... 158

LADIES and gentlemen, come to
    supper 101
Lady bird, lady bird, fly away home 57
Lady-bug, lady-bug............. 74
Lavender blue and Rosemary green 150
Lazy Tom, with jacket blue...... 137
Leg over leg 80
Lend me thy mare to ride a mile.. 99
"Let us go to the woods," says
    Richard to Robin........... 58
Little Betty Blue............... 158
*Little Betty Winkle, she had a lit-
    tle pig................... 29
Little Blue Betty lived in a lane... 101
Little Bob Robbin, where do you
    live? 134
Little Bob Snooks was fond of his
    books 108
Little Bo Peep has lost her sheep.. 110
Little Boy Blue, come blow your horn 86
Little Cock Robin peeped out of his
    cabin 99
Little drops of water........... 160
Little girl, little girl, where have
    you been? 94
Little Jack-a-Dandy 109
Little Jack Dandy-prat was my first
    suitor 94
*Little Jack Horner............ 24
Little Jack Jelf 68
Little Jack Jingle 62
Little Jack Nory 43
Little King Boggen he build a fine
    hall 169

Little lad, little lad............. 156
Little maid, little maid.......... 126
Little maid, pretty maid......... 151
Little Miss Donnet 66
Little Miss Lily 43
Little Miss Muffett 70
Little Poll Parrot 162
Little Polly Flinders........... 54
Little Queen Pippin 131
Little Robin Red-breast sat upon a
    hurdle 46
Little Robin Red-breast sat upon a
    rail 70
Little Robin Red-breast sat upon a
    tree 166
Little Tee Wee 143
Little Tommy Grace 35
Little Tommy Tittlemouse....... 149
*Little Tom Tucker........... 23
Little Tom Twig............. 83
London Bridge is broken down... 89
Love your own, kiss your own.... 119
Lucy Locket lost her pocket...... 133

MARCH winds and April show-
    ers 162
Margaret wrote a letter......... 165
Margery Mutton-pie and Johnny
    Bo-peep 112
Mary had a little lamb 114
Mary had a pretty bird 147
Mary, Mary, quite contrary..... 130
Master I have and I am his man.. 59
Matthew, Mark, Luke, and John. 125
May I have the pleasure to intro-
    duce xvi
Merry are the bells........... 81
Miss one, two, and three could
    never agree 137

Miss Jane had a bag............ 112
Mister East gave a feast......... 61
Molly, my sister and I fell out.... 61
Monday alone 83
Monday's bairn is fair of face.... 89
Moss was a little man.......... 162
Mrs. Bond, she went down to the
    pond in a rage............ 51
Multiplication is vexation....... 107
My aunt, she lost her petticoat.... 150
My dear, do you know........ 48
My father, he died........... 145
My father left me three acres of
    land 52
My grandmother sent me........ 87
My Lady Wind 53
My little old man and I fell out... 143
My maid Mary, she minds the dairy 68
My mother, and your mother..... 54
My pussy-cat has got the gout.... 80
My story's ended 42

NANCY Dawson has grown so
    fine 65
Needles and pins.............. 137
Nixie, Dixie, hickory bow........ 68
Noah of old did build an Ark..... 91
Nose, nose, jolly red nose........ 43
Now go to sleep, my little son.... 33
Now what do you think of Little
    Jack Jingle? 51

OF all the gay birds that e'er I
    did see 49
Oh, dear! What can the matter be?
    Two old women............ 89
Oh, dear! What can the matter be?
    Johnny's so long........... 57

Oh, the little rusty, dusty, rusty Miller ... 87
Old Boniface, he loved good cheer . 145
Old Father Grey Beard ... 142
Old Grimes is dead ... 63
Old King Cole was a merry old soul 151
Old woman, old woman, shall we go a-shearing? ... 133
Old Mistress McShuttle ... 62
Old Mother Goose when she wanted to wander ... 32
Old Mother Hubbard ... 127
Old Toby Sizer is such a miser ... 172
O, mother! I shall be married ... 90
*O, my kitten, my kitten ... 20
Once in my life, I married a wife ... 160
Once I saw a little bird ... 107
One, he loves; two, he loves ... 47
One for the money ... 146
One misty, moisty morning ... 37
Onery, ooery, ickery Ann ... 150
One-ery, You-ery, E-kery, Haven. 149
One old Oxford ox opening oysters. 85
One, two, buckle my shoe ... 92
One, two, three, I love coffee ... 62
One, two, three, four, Mary at the cottage door ... 47
One, two, three, four, five, catching fishes all alive ... 47
*1, 2, 3, 4, 5! I caught a hare alive. 31
On Saturday night it shall be my whole care ... 160
O! that I was where I would be ... 145
O, the grand old Duke of York ... 73
Over the water, and over the sea ... 87

*PEASE-PORRIDGE hot ... 22-118
Peg, peg, with a wooden leg ... 137
Peter, Peter, pumpkin eater ... 80

Peter Piper picked a peck ... 80
Peter White will ne'er go right ... 129
Phoebe rode a nanny-goat ... 96
Pickeleem, pickeleem pummis-stone. 105
Pinching, plodding Peter Clide ... 172
*Piping hot, smoking hot ... 24
Pit, pat, well-a-day ... 79
Pitty Patty Polt ... 99
Play, play every day ... 115
Please to remember ... 79
Polly, put the kettle on ... 60
Polly put the kettle on, Susy took it off ... 74
Polly, Dolly, Kate and Molly ... 171
Poor Dog Bright ... 79
Poor old Robinson Crusoe ... 98
Pretty John Watts ... 155
Punch and Judy ... 48
Pussy-cat ate the dumplings ... 66
Pussy Cat Mole ... 138
Pussy-Cat, pussy-cat, where have you been? ... 42
Pussy-Cat, wussy-cat, with a white foot ... 79
Pussy sits by the fire ... 75

QUIXOTE Quicksight ... 77

RABBIT, Rabbit, Rabbit Pie! ... 43
Rain, rain, go away ... 98
Rain, rain, go to Spain ... 38
Ride a cock-horse to Banbury Cross to see a fine lady ... 129
*Ride a cock-horse to Banbury Cross to see what Johnny can buy 24
Ride a cock-horse to Shrewsbury Cross ... 162

Riddle me, riddle me, ree ... 139
Ride, baby, ride ... 62
Ring-a-ring-a roses ... 170
Ring the bell! ... 167
Robert Barnes, fellow fine ... 79
Robert Rowley rolled a round roll round ... 92
Robin-a-bobbin ... 155
*Robin and Richard were two pretty men ... 26-33
Robin Hood, Robin Hood ... 140
Robin the Bobbin, the big-bellied Ben ... 88
Rock-a-bye, baby, thy cradle is green ... 98
Rosemary green, and lavender blue. 138
*Round about, round about, Magotty-pie ... 24
Rowley Powley, pudding and pie ... 150
Rub-a-dub-dub ... 48
Rumsey Dumsey's come to town ... 172

SAW ye aught of my love a-coming from the market ... 51
See a pin and pick it up ... 98
See-saw Jack in the hedge ... 104
*See-saw, Margery Daw, Jacky shall have a new master ... 25
See-saw, Margery Daw, Jennie shall have a new master ... 138
See-saw, Margery Daw, the old hen flew over ... 147
*See-saw, sacradown, sacradown ... 20
See, see. What shall I see? ... 135
*Shoe the colt ... 22
Shoe the horse and shoe the mare ... 137
Shoe the wild horse, and shoe the gray mare ... 155

Sieve my lady's oatmeal......... 147
Simple Simon met a pieman...... 167
Sing a song of sixpence.......... 68
Sing, sing! What shall I sing?... 123
Sing song! merry go 'round...... 134
Sleep, baby, sleep.............. 98
Smiling girls, rosy boys......... 79
Snail, snail, come out of your hole. 142
Snail, snail, come put out your horn 34
Sneeze on Monday, sneeze for danger 110
Solomon Grundy 99
Some little mice sat in a barn to spin 140
Speak when you're spoken to..... 86
St. Swithin's Day, if thou dost rain. 51
Swan, swam over the sea........ 39

TAFFY was a Welshman..... 96
*Tell-tale-tit! 23
Ten little Injuns standing in a line. 67
Thatcher of Thatchwood........ 159
The cock doth crow............ 97
The cock's on the housetop blowing his horn 49
The courtship and marriage of Cock Robin and Jenny Wren... 152
The cuckoo's a fine bird.......... 79
The dog will come when he is called 82
The dove says, "Coo, coo, what shall I do?" 79
The fair maid who, the first of May 88
The first day of Christmas....116-117
The fox and his wife had a great strife 113
The girl in the lane, that couldn't speak plain 36
The greedy man is he who sits.... 160
The hart he loves the high wood.. 115
The King of France went up the hill 49

The lion and the unicorn......... 148
The man in the moon came tumbling down 55
The man in the moon looked out of the moon 66
The man in the wilderness asked me 142
The miller, he grinds his corn..... 38
The North wind doth blow....... 101
The old woman must stand at the tub 158
The Queen of Hearts........... 97
The rose is red, the grass is green.. 101
The rose is red, the violet is blue.. 104
*The sow came in with the saddle. 29
The two gray kits.............. 118
The winds they did blow........ 147
There dwelt an old woman at Exeter 57
There was a crooked man........ 125
There was a fat man of Bombay.. 137
There was a frog lived in a well... 64
There was a jolly miller......... 34
There was a king met a king...... 49
There was a little boy and a little girl 114
There was a little girl who had a little curl 57
There was a little girl who wore a little hood 66
There was a little Guinea-pig..... 125
There was a little man and he had a little gun 166
*There was a little man and he wooed a little maid........... 27
There was a little nobby colt...... 155
There was a little one-eyed gunner. 94
There was a little woman as I've been told 70
There was a maid on Scrabble Hill. 144

There was a man and he had naught 151
There was a man and he was mad.. 125
There was a man and his name was Dob 155
There was a man in our town, he couldn't pay his rent........... 73
There was a man in our town and he was wondrous wise........ 94
*There was a man in Thessaly.... 23
There was a monkey........... 165
There was an idle boy........... 90
There was an old crow.......... 164
*There was an old man and he had a calf 30
*There was an old man in a velvet coat 25
There was an old man of Tobago.. 80
There was an old man who lived in a wood.................... 168
There was an old soldier of Bister. 103
*There was an old woman and she sold puddings and pies........ 30
There was an old woman, and what do think.................... 63
There was an old woman, as I've heard tell.................... 102
There was an old woman and nothing she had................. 171
There was an old woman called nothing at all............... 123
There was an old woman had three cows 36
There was an old woman had three sons 59
There was an old woman, her name it was Peg.................. 35
There was an old woman in Surrey. 70
*There was an old woman lived under a hill, and if she's not gone. 28

*There was an old woman lived under a hill, she put a mouse in a bag 28
There was an old woman of Gloucester 67
There was an old woman of Harrow 63
There was an old woman of Leeds. 74
There was an old woman tossed up in a basket................... 135
There was an old woman who lived in a shoe.................. 50
There was an old woman who rode on a broom.................. 139
There was an old woman sat spinning 161
There was an owl lived in an oak.. 65
There was a Piper had a cow..... 75
There was a rat for want of stairs. 90
There once were two cats of Kilkenny 52
There's a neat little clock........ 49
There were three jovial Welchmen. 164
*There were two birds sat upon a stone 26
*There were two blackbirds...... 28
There were two blind men....... 150
They that wash on Monday...... 107
Thirty days hath September...... 55
This is the house that Jack built... 95
This is the way the ladies ride..... 67
This pig went to the barn....... 52
Thomas A'Tattamus took two T's. 77
Three Blind Mice............. 44
*Three children sliding on the ice.. 21
Three little kittens they lost their mittens 126
Three straws on a staff.......... 75
*Three wise men of Gotham...30-132
Tip, top, tower................ 43
Tit, tat, toe.................. 49

To make your candles last forever. 142
To market, to market a gallop, a trot 130
To market, to market, to buy a fat pig 150
To market, to market, to buy a plum cake 112
To market ride the gentlemen.... 52
Tom, he was a Piper's son....... 60
Tommy kept a chandler's shop.... 80
Tommy's tears 161
Tommy Trot, a man of laws..... 143
Tom, Tom, the Piper's son, learned to play when he was young..... 123
Tom, Tom, the Piper's son, stole a pig 59
Toss up my darling............. 146
Trip and go, heave and ho....... 139
*Trip upon trenchers and dance upon dishes 28
Tweedle-dum and tweedle-dee.... 62
Twinkle, twinkle, little star.... 56
Two little dogs 139
Two little kittens, one stormy night. 41
Two monkeys came from native wood 70

UP at Piccadilly, oh!......... 63
Up by the chimney there is a small man 87
Up hill and down dale.......... 118
Up hill spare me............... 61
Upon my word and honor....... 141
Upon St. Paul's steeple stands a tree 53
Up street, and down street....... 112

WAS ever heard such noise and clamor 56

Wash me, and comb me......... 77
Wash the dishes............... 156
Wasn't it funny............... 170
We are all in the dumps........ 146
Wear you a hat, or wear you a crown 85
Wee Willie Winkie............. 61
We're all jolly boys............. 77
*We're three brethren out of Spain 22
What are little boys made of..... 151
*What care I how black I be..... 24
What do they call you?.......... 156
What's the news of the day?..... 66
What is the rhyme for porringer.. 78
When a twister a-twisting....... 75
When good King Arthur ruled his land 146
*When I was a bachelor, I lived by myself 21
*When I was a little boy, I had but little wit 30
When I was a little girl about seven years old 41
When I was a little girl, I washed my mammy's dishes.......... 104
When Jacky's a very good boy.... 83
When little Fred went to bed..... 170
When the days begin to lengthen.. 49
When the wind is in the east...... 70
When V and I together meet..... 127
Where are you going, my pretty maid? 78
Where have you been all the day?. 77
Where should a baby rest?....... 130
Where was a jewel and pretty.... 108
Whistle, daughter, whistle....... 168
*Who comes here?............. 22
Who ever saw a rabbit.......... 166
Who killed Cock Robin?........ 140

Why is pussy in bed, pray?........ 130
"Will you walk into my parlor"?.. 45
Willy boy, Willy boy........... 143
Willy, Willy Wilkin............ 65
Wooley Foster has gone to sea.... 42

YANKEE Doodle went to town. 148
Yaup, yaup, yaup!............ 104
Yeow mussent sing a' Sunday..... 99
Young lambs to sell........... 139
Young Roger came tapping at Dolly's window 65
You shall have an apple........ 108

Games and Riddles

A HILL full, a hole full...... 118
A riddle, a riddle............. 128
As high as a castle............ 39
As I was going o'er London Bridge 166
As I was going over Westminster Bridge 150
As I was going to St. Ives........ 123
As I went over the Lincoln Bridge. 39
As I went through the garden gap. 88
As round as an apple, as deep as a cup 148
As soft as silk, as white as milk.... 106
A water there is............... 160

BLACK within, and red without. 142
Black are we, but much admired... 102
Buff says Buff to all his men...... 60

DAFFY Down Dilly........ 94
Dance, Thumbkin, dance....... 163

EYE Winker 102

FLOUR of England......... 108
Formed long ago, yet made to-day. 92

GOOD horses, bad horses..... 35

HE loves me;—He don't...... 115
Humpty Dumpty 143
Here sits the Lord Mayor........ 90
Here we go 'round the mulberry bush 85
Hick-a-more, Hack-a-more....... 112
Higher than a house, higher than a tree 92
Higgledy, piddledy, here we lie... 108
How many miles is it to Babylon?. 33

I am a gold lock.............. 161
I charge my daughters, every one.. 156
I have a little sister, they call her Peep, Peep 87
I love my love with an A........ 106
I am become of flesh and blood.... 146
I'm in every one's way.......... 134
In marble walls as white as milk... 128
I've seen you where you never were 170
I went to the wood and got it..... 105
I went up one pair of stairs....... 97

LITTLE Nancy Etticote...... 88
Long legs, crooked thighs....... 155

MADE in London........... 170
Make three-fourths of a cross.... 57

NATURE requires five....... 35

OLD Mother Twitchet....... 149
One to make ready............. 51
One for the money, two for the show 146
Over the water................. 75

*PAT-A-CAKE, pat-a-cake, baker's man! 31
Purple, yellow, red, and green.... 57

RIDDLE-me, riddle-me, riddle-me-ree 34
Riddle me, riddle me, what is that? 149

THE calf, the goose, the bee... 85
The land was white........... 109
There was a girl in our town...... 98
There was a little green house..... 66
There was a man rode through our town 92
There was a man who had no eyes. 63
Thirty white horses............. 133
*This little pig went to market.... 25
Twelve pears hanging high....... 129
Two legs sat upon three legs..... 75

WE are three brethren out of Spain 159
What God never sees........... 57
What shoemaker makes shoes without leather.................. 151
When I was taken from the fair body 170
Who is going round my sheepfold? 55

A List of the Pictures

FOLLOWING PAGE

Little Jack Horner sat in a corner 24

One foot up, the other foot down. 26

Hush-a-bye, baby, on the treetop 26

Jack fell down and broke his crown 26

There was an old woman who lived in
a shoe 26

Little Miss Muffett sat on a tuffett 58

Peter, Peter, pumpkin-eater 58

Rain, rain, go away 58

Little Bo-Peep has lost her sheep. 58

FOLLOWING PAGE

Polly, put the kettle on, Polly, put the
kettle on 60

Hot cross buns, hot cross buns 88

Pease porridge hot, pease porridge cold 118

Mary, Mary, quite contrary 148

See-saw, Margery Daw. 148

Curly locks! curly locks! wilt thou be
mine 148

Ring a-round a rosie. 148

A dillar, a dollar, a ten o'clock scholar 150

"MAY I have the pleasure to introduce
Some very old friends," says Mother
Goose.

"There is little Bo Peep and little Boy Blue
And the little Old Woman who lived in a shoe,

Old Mother Hubbard, as well as her dog,
Dame Trot, and Sir Anthony Rowley Frog,

Humpty Dumpty, and Dickory Dock,
The dear little Mouse who ran up the clock,

The Puss who journeyed to London alone,
And saw the queen on a golden throne:

So come, my little folks, open me,
And lots of other old friends you'll see!"

THE FOLLOWING FIFTY-ONE RHYMES,
WITH THE MORALS, ARE ALL THAT
APPEARED IN THE FIRST KNOWN
EDITION OF MOTHER GOOSE RHYMES

BOW-WOW-WOW,
   Whose dog art thou?
Little Tom Tucker's dog,
Bow-wow-wow.
MORAL:
   Tom Tucker's dog is a very good dog and an honester dog than his master.

BOYS and girls, come out to play,
   The moon doth shine as bright as day;
Leave your supper, and leave your sleep,
And come with your playfellows into the street.
Come with a whoop, come with a call,
And come with a good will or come not at all.
Up the ladder and down the wall,
A halfpenny loaf will serve us all.
But when the loaf is gone, what will you do?
Those who must eat must work.
MORAL:
   All work and no play makes Jack a dull boy.

IS John Smith within?
   Yes, that he is.
Can he set a shoe?
Aye, marry, too.
   Here a nail,
   There a nail,
Tick, tack, too.
MORAL:
   Knowledge is a treasure, but practice is the way to it.

HERE'S A, B, C, D, E, F, and G, and
   H, I, J, K, L, M, N, O, P,
Q, R, S, T, U, V, W, X, Y, and Z;
And here the child's Dad,
Who is wise and discerning,
And knows this is the fount of learning.
MORAL:
   This is the most learned ditty in the world, for indeed there is no song written without the aid of it, for it is the gamut and groundwork of them all.

JACK Spratt could eat no fat,
　　His wife could eat no lean,
And so, betwixt them both, you see,
They licked the platter clean.
MORAL:
　　Better to go to bed supperless than to rise in debt.

BAA, baa, black sheep,
　　Have you any wool?
Yes sir, yes sir,
Three bags full:
One for the master,
One for the dame,
But none for the little boy
Who cries in the lane.
MORAL:
　　Bad habits are easier conquered to-day than to-mor-
row.

SEE-SAW, sacaradown, sacaradown,
　　Which is the way to London town?
One foot up, and the other foot down,
That is the way to London town.
MORAL:
　　Or to any town on the face of the earth.

O, MY kitten, my kitten,
　　And O, my kitten, my deary!
Such a sweet pet as this
　　Was neither far nor neary.

And here we go up, up, up,
　　And here we go down, down, down,
And here we go backwards and forwards,
　　And here we go round, round, round.
MORAL:
　　Idleness hath no advocate but many friends.

A LONG-TAILED pig, or a short-tailed pig,
　　Or a pig without e'er a tail,
A sow-pig, or a boar-pig,
　　Or a pig with a curly tail.
MORAL:
　　　　Take hold of his tail,
　　　　　And eat off his head,
　　　　And then you will be sure
　　　　　The pig-hog is dead.

WHEN I was a bachelor, I lived by myself,
    And all the bread and cheese I got I put
    upon a shelf;
The rats and the mice did lead me such a life,
That I went to market, to get myself a wife.

The streets were so broad, and the lanes were
    so narrow,
I could not get my wife home without a wheel-
    barrow:
The wheel-barrow broke, my wife got a fall,
Down tumbled wheel-barrow, little wife, and
    all.

MORAL:
    Provide against the world, and hope for the best.

THREE children sliding on the ice
    Upon a summer's day,
As it fell out, they all fell in—
    The rest they ran away.

Now had these children been at home,
    Or sliding on dry ground,
Ten thousand pounds to one penny,
    They had not all been drown'd.

Ye parents who have children dear,
    And eke ye that have none,
If you would keep them safe abroad,
    Pray keep them safe at home.

MORAL:
    There is something so melancholy in this song
that it has occasioned many people to weep. It is
almost as diuretic as the tune which John the coachman whistles to his horses.

I WOULD if I cou'd
    If I cou'dn't, how cou'd I?
I cou'dn't, unless I cou'd, cou'd I?
Cou'd you, without you cou'd, cou'd ye?
Cou'd you, cou'd ye?
Cou'd you, unless you cou'd, cou'd ye?

MORAL:
    This is a new way of handling an old argument,
said to be invented by a famous senator; but it has
something in it of Gothic construction.

SHOE the colt,
  Shoe the colt,
Shoe the wild mare;
  Here a nail,
  There a nail,
Yet she goes bare.

MORAL:
  Aye, Aye, drive the nail that will go.   That is the
way of the world and is the method pursued by all
our financiers, politicians, and necromancers.

WE'RE three brethren out of Spain
  Come to court your daughter Jane;
My daughter Jane, she is too young,
She has no skill in a flattering tongue.
It's for her gold she must be sold;
So fare you well, my lady gay,
We must return another day.

MORAL:
  Riches serve a wise man and govern a fool.

PEASE-porridge hot,
  Pease-porridge cold,
Pease-porridge in the pot,
Nine days old.
Spell me that in four letters.
I will.
T-H-A-T.

MORAL:
  The poor are seldomer sick for want of food than
the rich are by the excess of it.

I WON'T be my father's Jack,
  I won't be my mother's Jill,
I will be the fiddler's wife,
And have music when I will.
T'other little tune,
T'other little tune,
Prythee, love, play me
T'other little tune.

MORAL:
  Those arts are the most valuable which are of the
greatest use.

WHO comes here?
  " A grenadier."
What do you want?
" A pot of beer."
Where is your money?
  "I've forgot."
Get you gone,
  You can't have a drop.

MORAL:
  Intemperance is attended with disease and idleness
with poverty.

DICKERY, dickery, dock;
  The mouse ran up the clock;
The clock struck One,
The mouse ran down,
Dickery, dickery, dock.

MORAL:
  Time stays for no man.

HUSH-a-bye, baby, on the tree top,
    When the wind blows, the cradle will
rock;
When the bough bends, the cradle will fall.
Down will come baby, cradle, and all.
MORAL:
    This may serve as a warning to the proud and
ambitious who climb so high that they generally fall
at last. —Content turns all it touches into gold.

TELL-tale tit!
    Your tongue shall be slit,
And all the dogs in the town
Shall have a little bit.
MORAL:
    Point not at the faults of others with a foul finger.

THERE was a man in Thessaly,
    And he was wondrous wise;
He jumped into a quickset hedge,
And scratched out both his eyes;
And when he saw his eyes were out,
With all his might and main
He jumped into another hedge,
And scratched them in again.
MORAL:
    How happy it was for the man to scratch his eyes
in again when they were scratched out! But he was
a blockhead or he would have kept himself away
from the hedge and not been scratched at all.

LITTLE Tommy Tucker
    Sings for his supper;
What shall he eat?
White bread and butter.
How shall he cut it
Without e'er a knife?
How will he be married
Without o'er a wife?

MORAL:
    To be married without a wife is a terrible thing and
to be married with a bad wife is something worse.
However, a good wife that sings well is the best musi-
cal instrument in the world.

WHAT care I how black I be,
  Twenty pounds will marry me;
If twenty won't, forty shall,
I am my mother's bouncing girl!

MORAL:

  If we do not flatter ourselves, the flattery of others would have no effect.

PIPING hot!
  Smoking hot!
What have I got you have not?
Hot gray peas, hot, hot, hot,
Hot gray peas, hot.

MORAL:

  There is more music in this song on a cold frosty night then ever the Sirens were possessed of who captivated Ulysses, and the effect sticks closer to the ribs.

HEIGH, diddle, diddle,
  The cat and the fiddle,
The cow jumped over the moon;
The little dog laughed
To see such sport,
And the dish ran away with the spoon.

MORAL:

  It must have been a little dog that laughed, for a great dog would be ashamed to laugh at such nonsense.

RIDE a cock-horse to Banbury Cross,
  To see what Tommy can buy;
A penny white loaf, and a penny white cake,
And a two-pennny apple pie.

MORAL:

  There's a good boy! Eat up your pie and hold your tongue, for silence is the sign of wisdom.

ROUND about, round about,
  Magotty-pie,
My father loves good ale,
  And so do I.

MORAL:

  Evil company makes the good bad and the bad worse.

LITTLE Jack Horner
  Sat in a corner,
Eating a Christmas pie;
He put in his thumb,
And pulled out a plum,
And said, "What a good boy am I!"

MORAL:

  Jack was a boy of excellent taste, as should appear by his pulling out a plum. It is, therefore, supposed that his father apprenticed him to a mince pie maker that he might improve his taste from week to week. None stand in so much need of good taste as a pastry cook.

Little Jack Horner sat in a corner Eating a Christmas pie.

(Page 24)

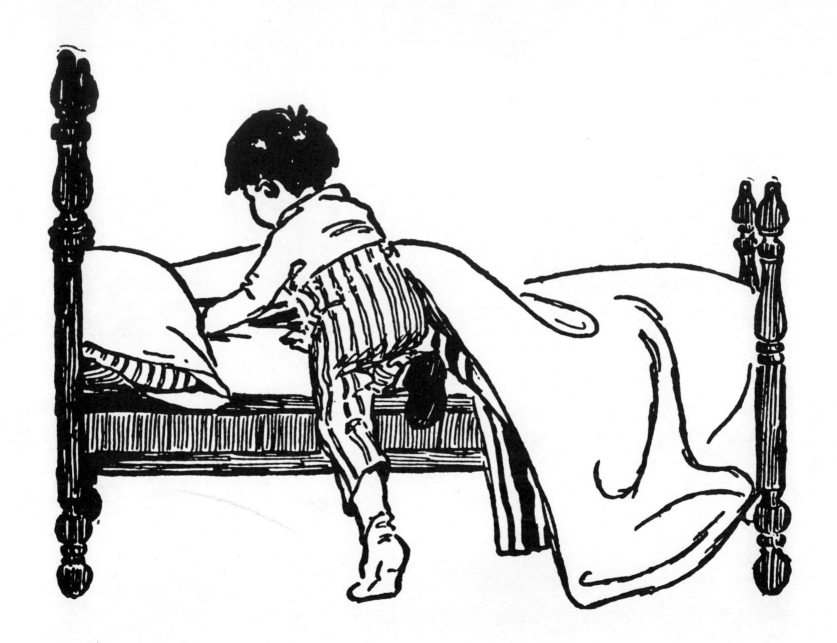

THERE was an old man in a velvet coat,
　　He kiss't a maid and gave her a groat;
The groat it was cracked and did not go.
Ah! old man, do you serve me so?
MORAL:
　　If the coat be ever so fine that a fool wears, it is still a fool's coat.

THIS little pig went to market.
　　This little pig stayed home.
This little pig had roast meat.
This little pig had none.
This little pig went to the barn door
And cried week, week, for more.
MORAL:
　　If we do not govern our passions, our passions will govern us.

SEE, saw, Margery Daw,
　　Jacky shall have a new master;
Jacky must have but a penny a day,
　　Because he can't work any faster.
MORAL:
　　It is a mean and scandalous practice of authors to put notes to things that deserve no notice.

GREAT A, little a,
　　Bouncing B!
The cat's in the cupboard,
　　And can't see me.
MORAL:
　　Yes, she can see that you are naughty and do not mind your book.

CROSS Patch,
   Draw the latch,
Sit by the fire and spin;
   Take a cup,
   And drink it up,
And call your neighbors in.

MORAL:
   A common case this, to call in our neighbors to
rejoice when all the good liquor is gone.

THERE were two birds sat upon a stone,
   Fal de ral-al de ral-laddy.
One flew away, and then there was one,
   Fal de ral-al de ral-laddy.
The other flew after, and then there was none,
   Fal de ral-al de ral-laddy.
So the poor stone was left all alone.
   Fal de ral-al de ral-laddy.
One of these little birds back again flew,
   Fal de ral-al de ral-laddy.
The other came after, and then there were two,
   Fal de ral-al de ral-laddy.
Says one to the other, pray how do you do?
   Fal de ral-al de ral-laddy.
Very well, thank you, and pray how are you?
   Fal de ral-al de ral-laddy.

MORAL:
   This may serve as a chapter of consequence in the
next book of logic.

ROBIN and Richard were two pretty men;
   They lay in bed till the clock struck ten;
Then up starts Robin, and looks in the sky,
Oh! brother Richard, the sun's very high!

MORAL:
   What lazy rogues are these to lie in bed so long.
I dare say they have no cloaks to their backs, for
laziness clothes a man with rags.

One foot up, the other foot down, and that is the way to London town.

(Page 20)

Hush-a-bye, baby, on the treetop, when the wind blows the cradle will r

Jack fell down and broke his crown, and Jill came tumbling after.

There was an old woman who lived in a shoe, she had so many children, she didn't know what to

THERE was a little man and he wooed a
  little maid,
And he said, "Little maid, will you wed—
  wed—wed;
I have little more to say than will you, yea or
  nay,
  For the least said is soonest mended, ded—
  ded—ded."

Then replied the little maid, "Sir, you've little
  said
To induce a little maid to wed—wed—wed;
You must say a little more and produce a little
  ore,
  E're I'll make a little print on your bed—
  bed—bed."

Then the little man replied, "If you'll be my
  little bride
I'll raise my love notes a little higher—
  higher—higher.
Though my offers are not mcct, yet my little
  heart is great,
  With the little God of Love on fire—fire—
  fire."

Then the little maid replied, some say a little
  sighed,
  "But what shall we have to eat—eat—eat;
Will the love that you're so rich in make the
  fire in the kitchen,
  Or the little God of Love turn the spit—
  spit—spit."

Then the little man replied, some say a little
  cried,
  For his little heart was big with sorrow—
  sorrow—sorrow,
"As I am your little slave, if the little that I have
  Be too little, little, we will borrow—borrow
  —borrow."

MORAL:
  He who borrows is another man's slave, and pawns
his honor, his liberty, and sometimes his nose for the
payment. Learn to live on little and be independent.

Then the little man so gent made the little
  maid relent
  And set her little heart a thinking—king—
  king,
Though his offers were but small, she took his
  little all,
  She could have but the cat and her skin—
  skin—skin.

THERE was an old woman lived under a
    hill,
And if she's not gone, she lives there still.
Baked apples she sold, and cranberry pies,
And she's the old woman that never told lies.

MORAL:
    This is a self-evident proposition which is the very
essence of truth.   None will presume to contradict
this.

THERE were two blackbirds
    Sitting on a hill.
The one named Jack,
    And the other named Jill,
Fly away, Jack!
Fly away, Jill!
Come again, Jack!
Come again, Jill!

MORAL:
    A bird in the hand is worth two in the bush.

TRIP upon trenchers, and dance upon dishes,
    My mother sent me for some bawn, some
bawn;
She bid me tread lightly, and come again
    quickly,
    For fear the young men should do me some
harm.
Yet didn't you see, yet didn't you see,
What naughty tricks they put upon me?
They broke my pitcher, and spilt the water,
And huffed my mother, and chid her daughter,
    And kissed my sister instead of me.

MORAL:
    What a succession of misfortunes befell this poor
girl?   But the last circumstance was the most affecting
and might have proved fatal.

THERE was an old woman
    Lived under a hill;
She put a mouse in a bag,
    And sent it to the mill.

The miller declar'd
    By the point of his knife,
He never took toll
    Of a mouse in his life.

MORAL:
    The only instance of a miller refusing toll and for
which the mouse has just cause for complaint against
him.

LITTLE Betty Winckle she had a little pig.
It was a little pig not very big;
When he was alive he lived in clover,
But now he is dead, and that's all over.
Johnny Winckle, he sate down and cried,
Betty Winckle, she laid down and died.
So there was an end of one, two, and three:
Johnny Winckle, He—
Betty Winckle, She—
And Piggy Wiggie—
MORAL:
A dirge is a song made for the dead, but whether this was made for Betty Winckle or her pig is uncertain; no notice being taken of it by Cambden or any of the famous antiquarians.
—*Wall's System of Sense.*

DING, dong, bell,
The cat is in the well!
Who put her in?
Little Johnny Green;
What a naughty boy was that
To try to drown poor pussy cat,
Who never did any harm,
And killed the mice in his father's barn.

MORAL:
He that injures one threatens a hundred.

THE sow came in with the saddle,
The little pig rock'd the cradle,
The dish jump'd up on the table,
To see the pot swallow the ladle.
The spit that stood behind the door
Threw the pudding-stick on the floor.
Odsplut! said the gridiron,
Can't you agree?
I'm the head constable,
Bring them to me.
MORAL:
If he acts as constable in this case, the cook must surely be the Justice of the Peace.

JACK and Jill went up the hill,
  To fetch a pail of water;
Jack fell down and broke his crown,
  And Jill came tumbling after.

Up Jack got and home did trot,
  As fast as he could caper;
Dame Jill had the job to plaster his knob,
  With vinegar and brown paper.
MORAL:
    The more we think of dying, the better we will live.

COCK a doodle doo!
  My dame has lost her shoe;
My master's lost his fiddling stick,
  And don't know what to do.
MORAL:
    The cock crows us up early in the morning that
we may work for our bread, and not live upon charity,
or upon trust, for he who lives upon charity shall be
often affronted, and he that lives upon trust shall pay
double.

THREE wise men of Gotham
  Went to sea in a bowl;
If the bowl had been stronger,
  My tale had been longer.
MORAL:
    It is long enough. Never lament the loss of what
is not worth having.

WHEN I was a little boy, I had but little
    wit,
It is some time ago, and I've no more yet;
Nor ever, ever shall, until I die,
For the longer I live, the more fool am I.
MORAL:
    He that will be his own master has often a fool for
his scholar.

THERE was an old man,
    And he had a calf,
  And that's half;
He took him out of the stall,
  And put him on the wall,
  And that's all.
MORAL:
    Those who are given to telling all they know gen-
erally tell more than they know.

THERE was an old woman,
    And she sold puddings and pies;
She went to the mill,
And the dust flew into her eyes.
Hot pies and cold pies to sell.
Wherever she goes you may follow her by
    the smell.
MORAL:
    Either say nothing of the absent or speak like a
friend.

PAT-A-CAKE, pat-a-cake, baker's man!
   Make me a cake as fast as you can:
Pat it, and prick it, and mark it with T,
And there will be enough for Baby and me.
MORAL:
   The surest way to gain our ends is to moderate our
desires.

1, 2, 3, 4, 5!
   I caught a hare alive;
6, 7, 8, 9, 10!
   I let him go again.
MORAL:
   We may be as good as we please if we please to be
good.

OLD MOTHER GOOSE

OLD Mother Goose, when
  She wanted to wander,
Would ride through the air
  On a very fine gander.

Mother Goose had a house,
  'Twas built in a wood,
Where an owl at the door
  For sentinel stood.

This is her son Jack,
  A plain-looking lad;
He is not very good,
  Nor yet very bad.

She sent him to market—
  A live goose he bought:
"Here, mother," says he,
  "It will not go for naught."

Jack's goose and her gander
  Grew very fond,
They'd both eat together,
  Or swim in one pond.

Jack found one fine morning,
  As I have been told,

His goose had laid him
  An egg of pure gold.

Jack rode to his mother,
  The news for to tell;
She called him a good boy
  And said it was well.

Jack sold his gold egg
  To a rascally knave,
Not half of its value
  To poor Jack he gave.

Then Jack went a-courting
  A lady so gay,
As fair as the lily,
  And sweet as the May.

The knave and the Squire
  Came up at his back,
And began to belabor
  The sides of poor Jack.

And then the gold egg
  Was thrown into the sea,
When Jack he jumped in,
  And got it back presently.

The knave got the goose,
  Which he vowed he would kill,
Resolving at once
  His pockets to fill.

Jack's mother came in,
  And caught the goose soon,
And mounting its back,
  Flew up to the moon.

But old Mother Goose
  That instant came in,
And turned her son Jack
  Into famed Harlequin.

She then with her wand
  Touched the lady so fine
And turned her at once
  Into sweet Columbine.

ROBIN and Richard are two pretty men,
  They laid in bed till the clock struck ten;
Then up starts Robin and looks in the sky,
"Oh, brother Richard, the sun's very high!
You go on with the bottle and bag,
And I'll come after with jolly Jack Nag."

[The following is a game played as follows: A string of boys and girls, each holding by his predecessor's skirts, approaches two others, who with joined and elevated hands form a double arch. After the dialogue, the line passes through, and the last is caught by a sudden lowering of the arms—if possible.]

HOW many miles is it to Babylon?
  Threescore miles and ten.
Can I get there by candle-light?
  Yes, and back again!
If your heels are nimble and light,
You may get there by candle-light.

I BOUGHT a dozen new-laid eggs,
  Of good old farmer Dickens;
I hobbled home upon two legs,
  And found them full of chickens.

AS I was going up and down,
  I met a little dandy,
He pulled my nose, and with two blows
  I knocked him down quite handy.

NOW go to sleep, my little son,
  Or I shall have to spank you;
How do you do? says uncle John—
  I'm pretty well, I thank you.

BRYAN O'Lin and his wife, and wife's
    mother,
They all went over the bridge together:
The bridge broke down, and they all fell in,—
The deuce go with all! said Bryan O'Lin.

AS Tommy Snooks and Bessy Brooks
    Were walking out one Sunday,
Says Tommy Snooks to Bessy Brooks,
    "To-morrow will be Monday."

SNAIL, snail, come put out your horn,
    To-morrow is the day to shear the corn.

RIDDLE-me riddle-me riddle-me-ree,
    Perhaps you can tell what this riddle
may be:
As deep as a house, as round as a cup,
And all the king's horses can't draw it up.
                [A well.]

THERE was a jolly miller
    Lived on the river Dee,
He look'd upon his pillow,
    And there he saw a flea.
Oh! Mr. Flea,
You have bitten me,
    And you must die;
So he crack'd his bones
Upon the stones,
    And there he let him lie.

DANCE, little baby, dance up high,
    Never mind, baby, mother is by;
Crow and caper, caper and crow,
There, little baby, there you go;
Up to the ceiling, down to the ground,
Backwards and forwards, round and round;
Dance, little baby, and mother will sing,
With the merry carol, ding, ding, ding!

BYE, baby, bumpkin,
   Where's Tony Lumpkin?
My lady's on her death-bed,
With eating half a pumpkin.

[Hours of Sleep.]

NATURE requires five,
   Custom gives seven,
Laziness takes nine,
   And wickedness eleven.

A MAN went a-hunting at Reigate,
   And wished to leap over a high gate.
Says the owner, "Go round,
With your dog and your hound,
For you never shall leap over my gate."

A SUNSHINE shower
   Won't last half-an-hour.
As the day lengthens,
So the cold strengthens.
The fishes' cry
Is never long dry.

CHARLEY Wag, Charley Wag,
   Ate the pudding, and left the bag.

A SWARM of bees in May
   Is worth a load of hay;
A swarm of bees in June
Is worth a silver spoon;
A swarm of bees in July
Is not worth a fly.

[The following lines are sung by children when starting for a race.]

GOOD horses, bad horses,
   What is the time of day?
Three o'clock, four o'clock,
   Now fare you away.

LITTLE Tommy Grace had a pain in his face,
   So bad he could not learn a letter;
When in came Dicky Long,
Singing such a funny song,
That Tommy laughed, and found his face
   much better.

THERE was an old woman, her name it
   was Peg;
Her head was of wood, and she wore a cork
   leg,
The neighbors all pitch'd her into the water,
Her leg was drown'd first, and her head follow'd a'ter.

THE girl, in the lane, that couldn't speak
Cried, "Gobble, gobble, gobble:" [plain,
The man on the hill, that couldn't stand still,
Went hobble, hobble, hobble.

A, B, C, and D,
Pray, playmates, agree.
E, F, and G,
Well, so it shall be.
H, I, J, K, and L,
In peace we will dwell
M, N, and O,
To play let us go.
P, Q, R, and S,
Love may we possess.
W, X, and Y,
Will not guard or die.
Z, and &
Go to school at command.

DANCE to your daddy,
My little babby;
Dance to your daddy,
My little lamb.

You shall have a fishy
In a little dishy;
You shall have a fishy
When the boat comes in.

THERE was an old woman had three cows,
Rosy, and Colin, and Dun;
Rosy and Colin were sold at the fair,
And Dun broke his head in a fit of despair;
And there was the end of her three cows,
Rosy, and Colin, and Dun;

JOHN Cook had a little gray mare; he, haw,
  hum!
Her back stood up, and her bones they were
  bare; he, haw, hum!

John Cook was riding up Shuter's bank; he,
  haw, hum!
And there his nag did kick and prank; he,
  haw, hum!

John Cook was riding up Shuter's hill; he,
  haw, hum!
His mare fell down, and she made her will;
  he, haw, hum!

The bridle and saddle were laid on the shelf;
  he, haw, hum!
If you want any more you may sing it your-
  self; he, haw, hum.

ONE misty, moisty morning,
  When cloudy was the weather,
I chanced to meet an old man clothed all in
  leather.
He began to compliment, and I began to grin,
  How do you do, and how do you do?
  And how do you do again?

HICKERY, dickery, 6 and 7,
  Alabone, crackabone, 10 and 11;
Spin, spun, muskidem,
Twiddle 'em, twaddle 'em, 21.

IF all the seas were one sea,
  What a *great* sea that would be!
And if all the trees were one tree,
What a *great* tree that would be!
And if all the axes were one axe,
What a *great* axe that would be!
And if all the men were one man,
What a *great* man he would be!
And if the *great* man took the *great* axe,
And cut down the *great* tree,
And let it fall into the *great* sea,
What a splish, splash *that* would be!

I HAD a little pony
  I call'd him Dapple Gray,
I lent him to a lady,
To ride a mile away.
She whipped him, she slashed
  him,
She rode him through the mire;
I would not lend my pony now,
For all the lady's hire.

A LITTLE cock sparrow sat on a green tree,
    And he chirruped, he chirruped, so merry
        was he;
A little cock sparrow sat on a green tree,
And he chirruped, he chirruped, so merry was
    he.

A naughty boy came with his wee bow and
    arrow,
Determined to shoot this little cock sparrow.
A naughty boy came with his wee bow and
    arrow,
Determined to shoot this little cock sparrow.

"This little cock sparrow will make me a stew,
And his giblets shall make me a little pie too."
"Oh, no!" said the sparrow, "I won't make a
    stew,"
And he flapped his wings and away he flew!

A-MILKING, a-milking, my maid.
    "Cow, take care of your heels," she said,
    "And you shall have some nice new hay,
If you'll quietly let me milk away."

R AIN, rain, go to Spain,
    Don't come back again!

T HE miller he grinds his corn, his corn;
    The miller he grinds his corn, his corn;
The little boy blue comes winding his horn,
    With a hop, step, and a jump.

The carter he whistles aside his team;
The carter he whistles aside his team;
And Dolly comes tripping with the nice clouted
        cream,
    With a hop, step, and a jump.

The nightingale sings when we're at rest;
The nightingale sings when we're at rest;
The little bird climbs the tree for his nest,
    With a hop, step, and a jump.

The damsels are churning for curds and whey;
The damsels are churning for curds and whey;
The lads in the field are making the hay,
    With a hop, step, and a jump.

A S Tittymouse sat in the witty to spin,
    Pussy came to her and bid her good e'en,
"Oh, what are you doing, my little 'oman?"
"A-spinning a doublet for my gude man."
"Then shall I come to thee and wind up thy
    thread?"
"Oh, no, Mr. Puss, you will bite off my head."

HARK! hark! the dogs do bark,
   The beggars have come to town;
Some in rags, and some in tags,
   And some in velvet gowns.

AS high as a castle,
   As weak as a wastle;
And all the king's horses
Cannot pull it down.
   [Smoke.]

FOR every evil under the sun,
   There is a remedy, or there is none.
If there be one, try and find it,
If there be none, never mind it.

GO to bed first, a golden purse;
   Go to bed second, a golden pheasant;
Go to bed third, a golden bird.

I HAD a little dog, his name was Buff,
   I sent him to the store for an ounce of snuff,
But he lost the bag, and spilt the snuff,
So take that cuff, and that's enough.

SWAN, swam over the sea;
   Swim, swan, swin.
Swan, swam back again;
Well, swum, swan.

AS I went over Lincoln Bridge,
   I met Mister Rusticap;
Pins and needles on his back,
A-going to Thorney Fair.
   [A Hedgehog.]

A was an Apple-pie:

B bit it;

C cut it;

D dealt it;

E eat it;

F fought for it;

G got it;

H had it;

I inspected it.

J jumped for it;

K kept it;

L longed for it.

M mourned for it;

N nodded at it;

O opened it;

P peeped in it;

Q quartered it;

R ran for it;

S stole it;

T took it;

U used it.

V viewed it;

W wanted it;

X, Y, Z, and &,
All wished for a piece in hand

CHARLEY Warley had a cow
Black and white about the brow,
Open the gate and let her through,
Charley Warley's old cow!

I DO not like thee, Dr. Fell,
The reason why I cannot tell;
But this I know, and know full well,
I do not like thee, Dr. Fell.

TWO little kittens, one stormy night,
 Began to quarrel and then to fight;
One had a mouse, and the other had none,
And that's the way the quarrel begun.

" I'll have that mouse," said the biggest cat.
" You'll have that mouse? We'll see about
 that !"
" I will have that mouse," said the eldest son.
" You shan't have the mouse," said the little
 one.

I told you before 'twas a stormy night
When these two little kittens began to fight;
The old woman seized her sweeping broom,
And swept the two kittens right out of the room.

The ground was covered with frost and snow,
And the two little kittens had nowhere to go;
So they laid them down on the mat at the door,
While the old woman finished sweeping the
 floor.

Then they crept in, as quiet as mice,
All wet with the snow, and as cold as ice,
For they found it was better, that stormy
 night,
To lie down and sleep than to quarrel and
 fight.

WHEN I was a little girl about seven years
 old,
I hadn't got a petticoat to cover me from the
 cold;
So I went into Darlington that pretty little
 town,
And there I bought a petticoat, a cloak, and a
 gown,
I went into tnc woods and built me a kirk,
And all the birds of the air, they helped me to
 work.
The hawk, with his long claws, pulled down
 the stone,
The dove, with her rough bill, brought me
 them home:
The parrot was the clergyman, the peacock
 was the clerk,
The bullfinch played the organ, and we made
 merry work.

MY story's ended,
My spoon is bended;
If you don't like it,
Go to the next door,
And get it mended.

PUSSY-CAT, pussy-cat, where have you
been?
I've been to London to visit the Queen!
Pussy-cat, pussy-cat, what did you there?
I frighten'd a little mouse under her chair.

WOOLEY Foster has gone to sea,
With silver buckles at his knee;
When he comes back he'll marry me—
Bonny Wooley Foster!

Wooley Foster has a cow,
Black and white about the mow;
Open the gates and let her through—
Wooley Foster's own cow!

Wooley Foster has a hen,
Cockle button, cockle ben;
She lays eggs for gentlemen—
But none for Wooley Foster!

BOSSY-COW, bossy-cow, where do you lie?
In the green meadow under the sky.

Billy-horse, billy-horse, where do you lie?
Out in the stable with nobody nigh.

Birdies bright, birdies sweet, where do you lie?
Up in the tree-tops,—oh, ever so high!

Baby dear, baby love, where do *you* lie?
In my warm crib, with Mamma close by.

IN April's sweet month,
   When the leaves 'gin to spring
Little lambs skip like fairies
And birds build and sing.

LITTLE Miss Lily, you're dreadfully silly
   To wear such a very long skirt:
If you take my advice, you would hold it up
And not let it trail in the dirt.   [nice

LITTLE Jack Nory
   Told me a story.
How he tried
Cock-horse to ride,
Sword and scabbard by his side,
Saddle, leaden spurs and switches,
   His pocket tight
   With pence all bright,
Marbles, tops, puzzles, props,
Now he's put in a jacket and breeches.

TIP, top, tower,
   Tumble down in an hour.

RABBIT, Rabbit, Rabbit Pie!
   Come, my ladies, come and buy;
Else your babies they will cry.

A PIE sate on a pear-tree,
   A pie sate on a pear-tree,
A pie sate on a pear-tree,
Heigh O, heigh O, heigh O!
Once so merrily hopped she,
Twice so merrily hopped she,
Thrice so merrily hopped she,
Heigh O, heigh O, heigh O!

A RED sky at night,
   Is the shepherd's delight.
A red sky in the morning,
Is the shepherd's warning.

AROUND the green gravel the grass grows
      green,
And all the pretty maids are plain to be seen;
Wash them with milk, and clothe them with
      silk,
And write their names with a pen and ink.

NOSE, nose, jolly red nose;
   And what gave thee that jolly red nose?
Nutmegs and cinnamon, spices and cloves,
And they gave me this jolly red nose.

AS I was going to market upon a market day,
I met the finest ram, sir, that ever fed on hay,
  On hay, on hay, on hay—
I met the finest ram, sir, that ever fed on hay.

This ram was fat behind, sir; this ram was fat before;
This ram was ten yards round, sir; indeed he was no more.
  No more, no more, no more—
This ram was ten yards round, sir; indeed he he was no more.

The horns grew on his head, sir, they were so wondrous high,
As I've been plainly told, sir, they reached up to the sky,
  The sky, the sky, the sky—
As I've been plainly told, sir, they reached up to the sky.

The tail grew on his back, sir, was six yards and an ell,
And it was sent to market to toll the market bell,
  The bell, the bell, the bell—
And it was sent to market to toll the market bell.

THREE Blind Mice,
     See how they run!
They all ran after the farmer's wife,
Who cut off their tails with a carving knife;
Did ever you hear such a thing in your life
     As three blind mice?

"WILL you walk into my parlor?" said the
spider to the fly;
"'Tis the prettiest little parlor that ever you did
spy.
The way into my parlor is up a winding stair;
And I have many curious things to show you
when you're there."
"Oh, no, no," said the little fly; "to ask me is
in vain;
For who goes up your winding stair can ne'er
come down again."

"I'm sure you must be weary, dear, with soar-
ing up so high;
Will you rest upon my little bed?" said the
spider to the fly.

"There are pretty curtains drawn around; the
sheets are fine and thin;
And if you like to rest awhile, I'll snugly tuck
you in!"
"Oh, no, no," said the little fly; "for I've often
heard it said,
They never, never wake again, who sleep upon
your bed!"

Said the cunning spider to the fly,—
"Dear friend, what can I do
To prove the warm affection I've always felt
for you?"
"I thank you, gentle sir," she said, "for what
you're pleased to say,
And bidding you good-morning now, I'll call
another day."

The spider turned him round about, and went
into his den,
For well he knew the silly fly would soon come
back again;
So he wove a subtle web in a little corner sly,
And set his table ready, to dine upon the fly.
Then he came out to his door again, and
merrily did sing,—
"Come hither, hither, pretty fly, with the pearl
and silver wing;

Your robes are green and purple, there's a
    crest upon your head!
Your eyes are like the diamond bright, but
    mine are dull as lead!"

Alas! alas! how very soon this silly little fly,
Hearing his wily, flattering words, came slowly
    flitting by.
With buzzing wings she hung aloft, then near
    and nearer drew,
Thinking only of her brilliant eyes, her green
    and purple hue,—
Thinking only of her crested head—poor
    foolish thing! At last,
Up jumped the cunning spider, and fiercely
    held her fast!
He dragged her up his winding stair, into his
    dismal den,
Within his little parlor,—but she ne'er came
    out again!

And now, dear little children, who may this
    story read,
To idle, silly, flattering words, I pray you ne'er
    give heed;
Unto an evil counsellor close heart and ear and
    eye,
And take a lesson from this tale of the Spider
    and the Fly.

BOBBY Shaftoe's gone to sea,
    Silver buckles on his knee;
He'll come back and marry me,
    Pretty Bobby Shaftoe.

Bobby Shaftoe's fat and fair,
Combing down his yellow hair;
He's my love for evermore;
    Pretty Bobby Shaftoe.

LITTLE Robin Red-breast
    Sat upon a hurdle,
With a pair of speckled legs,
    And a green girdle.

DARBY and Joan were dress'd in black,
    Sword and buckle behind their back;
Foot for foot, and knee for knee,
Turn about Darby's company.

AN old woman lived in Nottingham town,
    Who owned a small house, and painted it
    brown;
And yet this old woman grew crazy with fright,
Lest some one should burn her house in the
    night.

"BILLY, Billy, come and play,
While the sun shines bright as day."

"Yes, my Polly, so I will,
For I love to please you still."

"Billy, Billy, have you seen
Sam and Betsy on the green?"

"Yes, my Poll, I saw them pass,
Skipping o'er the new-mown grass."

"Billy, Billy, come along,
And I will sing a pretty song."

BRYAN O'Lin had no breeches to wear,
So he bought him a sheepskin and made
him a pair.
With the skinny side out, and the woolly side in,
"Ah ha, that is warm!" said Bryan O'Lin.

ONE, two, three, four, five,
Catching fishes all alive.
Why did you let them go?
Because they bit my finger so.
Which finger did they bite?
The little finger on the right.

ONE, two, three, four,
Mary at the cottage door;
Five, six, seven, eight,
Eating cherries off a plate;
O-U-T spells out!

ONE, he loves; two, he loves;
Three, he loves, they say;
Four, he loves with all his heart;
Five, he casts away.
Six, he loves; seven, she loves;
Eight, they both love.
Nine, he comes; ten, he tarries;
Eleven, he courts; twelve, he marries.

MY dear, do you know,
How a long time ago,
Two poor little children,
Whose names I don't know,
Were stolen away on a fine summer's day,
And left in a wood, as I've heard people say.

And when it was night,
So sad was their plight,
The sun it went down,
And the moon gave no light!
They sobbed, and they sighed, and they bitterly
cried,
And the poor little things, they lay down and
died.

And when they were dead,
The robins so red

Brought strawberry leaves,
And over them spread;
And all the day long,
They sung them this song:
"Poor babes in the wood! poor babes in the
wood!
And don't you remember the babes in the
wood?"

PUNCH and Judy
Fought for a pie,
Punch gave Judy
A knock in the eye.

Says Punch to Judy,
"Will you have any more?"
Says Judy to Punch,
"My eyes are too sore."

RUB-A-DUB-DUB,
Three men in a tub;
And who do you think they be?
The butcher, the baker,
The candlestick-maker;
Turn 'em out, knaves all three!

THE King of France went up the hill
  With twenty thousand men;
The King of France came down the hill,
  And ne'er went up again.

TIT, tat, toe,
  My first go,
Three jolly butcher boys
All in a row;
Stick one up,
Stick one down,
Stick one on the old man's crown.

THERE'S a neat little clock,
  In the schoolroom it stands,
And it points to the time
  With its two little hands.

And may we, like the clock,
  Keep a face clean and bright,
With hands ever ready
  To do what is right.

WHEN the days begin to lengthen
  The cold begins to strengthen.

OF all the gay birds that e'er I did see,
  The owl is the fairest by far to me;
For all the day long she sits on a tree,
And when the night comes, away flies she.

THERE was a king met a king
  In a narrow lane;
Says this king to that king,
  "Where have you been?"

Oh! I've been a-hunting
  With my dog and my doe.
"Pray lend him to me,
  That I may do so."

There's the dog—take the dog.
  "What's the dog's name?"
I've told you already.
  "Pray tell me again."

THE cock's on the housetop blowing his
    horn;
The bull's in the barn a-threshing of corn;
The maids in the meadows are making of hay;
The ducks in the river are swimming away.

THERE was an old woman who lived in a
      shoe,
She had so many children, she didn't know
      what to do.
She gave them some broth, without any
      bread,
She whipped them all round, and sent them to
      bed,

I SAW a ship a-sailing,
    A sailing on the sea;
And, oh! it was all laden
    With pretty things for thee!

There were comfits in the cabin,
    And apples in the hold!
The sails were made of silk,
    And the masts were made of gold.

The four-and-twenty sailors,
    That stood between the decks,
Were four-and-twenty white mice,
    With chains about their necks.

The Captain was a duck,
    With a packet on his back;
And when the ship began to move,
    The captain said, "Quack! Quack!"

DID you see my wife, did you see, did you
      see,
    Did you see my wife looking for me?
She wears a straw bonnet, with white ribbons
      on it,
    And dimity petticoats over her knee.

COME, my children, come away,
    For the sun shines bright to-day;
Little children, come with me,
Birds and brooks and posies see;
Get your hats and come away,
For it is a pleasant day.

Everything is laughing, singing,
All the pretty flowers are springing;
See the kitten, full of fun,
Sporting in the brilliant sun;
Children too may sport and play,
For it is a pleasant day.

Bring the hoop, and bring the ball,
Come with happy faces all;
Let us make a merry ring,
Talk and laugh, and dance and sing.
Quickly, quickly, come away,
For it is a pleasant day.

CUSHY cow bonny,
  Let down thy milk,
And I will give thee a gown of silk;
A gown of silk and a silver tee,
If thou wilt let down thy milk to me.

"COME, let's to bed,"
  Says Sleepy-head;
"Tarry a while," says Slow.
"Put on the pot,"
Says the Greedy one,
"Let's sup before we go."

NOW what do you think
  Of little Jack Jingle?
Before he was married
  He used to live single.

MRS. Bond she went down to the pond in
    a rage,
With plenty of onions, and plenty of sage;
She cried, "Come, little wag-tails, come and be
    killed,
For you shall be stuffed, and my customers
    filled!"

ONE to make ready,
  And two to prepare,
Good luck to the rider,
  And away goes the mare.

SAW ye aught of my love a-coming from the
    market;
  A peck of meal upon her back,
  A babby in her basket?
Saw ye aught of my love coming from the
    market?

ST. SWITHIN'S day, if thou dost rain,
  For forty days it will remain;
St. Swithin's day, if thou be fair,
For forty days 'twill rain na mair.

MY father left me three acres of land,
   Sing ivy, sing ivy,
My father left me three acres of land,
   Sing holly, go whistle, and ivy!

I ploughed it with a ram's horn,
   Sing ivy, sing ivy;
And sowed it all over with one peppercorn,
   Sing holly, go whistle, and ivy!

I harrowed it with a bramble bush,
   Sing ivy, sing ivy;
And reaped it with my little penknife,
   Sing holly, go whistle, and ivy!

I got the mice to carry it to the barn,
   Sing ivy, sing ivy;
And thrashed it with a goose's quill,
   Sing holly, go whistle, and ivy!

I got the cat to carry it to the mill,
   Sing ivy, sing ivy;
The miller he swore he would have her paw,
And the cat she swore she would scratch his
     face,
   Sing holly, go whistle, and ivy!

THERE once were two cats of Kilkenny,
   Each thought there was one cat too many,
So they fought and they fit,
And they scratched and they bit,
Till, excepting their nails
And the tips of their tails,
Instead of two cats, there weren't any.

1 This pig went to the barn;
2 This ate all the corn;
3 This said he would tell;
4 This said he wasn't well;
5 This went week, week, week,
    over the door sill.

TO market ride the gentlemen,
   So do we, so do we;
Then comes the country clown,
   Hobbledy gee, Hobbledy gee;
First go the ladies, nim, nim, nim;
Next come the gentlemen, trim, trim, trim, trim,
Then come the country clowns, gallop-a-trot.

GO to bed Tom, go to bed Tom,
   Merry or sober, go to bed Tom.

MY Lady Wind, my Lady Wind,
  Went round about the house to find
  A chink to get her foot in.
She tried the key-hole in the door,
She tried the crevice in the floor,
  And drove the chimney soot in.

And then one night when it was dark
She blew up such a tiny spark,
  That all the house was bothered:
From it she raised up such a flame,
As flamed away to Belting Lane,
  And White Cross folks were smothered

And thus when once, my little dears,
A whisper reaches itching ears,
  The same will come, you'll find:
Take my advice, restrain the tongue,
Remember what old Nurse has sung
  Of busy Lady Wind!

UPON St. Paul's steeple stands a tree,
  As full of apples as may be.
The little boys of London town,
They run with hooks and pull them down;
And then they run from hedge to hedge
Until they come to London Bridge.

A LITTLE cock sparrow sat on a tree,
  Looking as happy as happy could be,
Till a boy came by with his bow and arrow,
Says he, I will shoot the little cock sparrow.

His body will make me a nice little stew,
And his giblets will make me a little pie, too.
Says the little cock sparrow, I'll be shot if stay,
So he clapped his wings, and fley away.

I LIKE little pussy,
  Her coat is so warm,
And if I don't hurt her,
  She'll do me no harm;
So I'll not pull her tail,
  Nor drive her away,
But pussy and I
  Very gently will play.

ELIZABETH, Elspeth, Betsy and Bess,
    They all went together to seek a bird's nest.
They found a bird's nest with five eggs in,
They all took one, and left four in.

LITTLE Polly Flinders
    Sat among the cinders,
  Warming her pretty little toes;
Her mother came and caught her,
And whipped her little daughter
    For spoiling her nice new clothes.

IF all the world was apple-pie,
    And all the sea was ink,
And all the trees were bread and cheese,
What should we have to drink?

I HAD a little husband, no bigger than my
        thumb;
I put him in a pint-pot, and there I bid him
        drum

I bought a little horse, that galloped up and
        down;
I saddled him and bridled him, and sent him
    out of town.

I gave him some garters, to garter up his
    hose,
And a little pocket handkerchief to wipe his
    pretty nose.

MY mother, and your mother,
        Went over the way;
Said my mother, to your mother,
"It's chop-a-nose day."

HUSH, baby, my doll, I pray you, don't cry,
        And I'll give you some bread, and some
        milk by-and-bye;
Or, perhaps, you like custard, or, maybe, a tart,
Then to either you are welcome, with all my
    heart.

IF I'd as much money as I could spend,
  I never would cry old chairs to mend;
Old chairs to mend, old chairs to mend;
I never would cry old chairs to mend.

If I'd as much money as I could tell,
I never would cry old clothes to sell;
Old clothes to sell; old clothes to sell;
I never would cry old clothes to sell.

AS I was going along long, long,
  A singing a comical song, song, song,
The lane that I went was so long, long, long,
And the song that I sung was so long, long,
    long.
And so I went singing along.

GOOSEY, goosey, gander, wither dost thou
    wander?
Up stairs, and down stairs, and in my lady's
    chamber.
There I met an old man, who would not say
    his prayers;
I took him by the left leg, and threw him
    down stairs.

THE man in the moon
  Came tumbling down,
And asked the way to Norwich.
He went by the South,
And he burnt his mouth,
With eating cold pease porridge.

[Two of the strongest children are selected, A and B; A stands within a ring of the children, B being outside.]

A. Who is going round my sheepfold;
B. Only poor old Jacky Lingo.
A. Don't steal any of my black sheep.
B. No, no more I will, only by one,
  Up, says Jacky Lingo.   (*Strikes one.*)

[The child struck leaves the ring, and takes hold of B behind; B in the same manner takes the other children, one by one, gradually increasing his tail on each repetition of the verses, until he has got the whole: A then tries to get them back; B runs away with them; they try to shelter themselves behind B; A drags them off, one by one, setting them against a wall, until he has recovered all. A regular tearing game, as children say.]

THIRTY days hath September,
  April, June, and November;
All the rest have thirty-one—
Except February, alone,
Which has four and twenty-four,
And every fourth year, one day more.

DEEDLE, deedle, dumpling, my son John,
  Went to bed with his stockings on;
One shoe off, and one shoe on,
Deedle, deedle, dumpling, my son John.

BUTTONS a farthing a pair,
  Come, who will buy them of me?
They're round and sound and pretty,
And fit for the girls of the city.
Come, who will buy them of me,
Buttons a farthing a pair?

FIDDLE-DE-DEE, fiddle-de-dee,
  The fly shall marry the humble-bee.
They went to the church, and married was she,
The fly has married the humble-bee.

TWINKLE, twinkle, little star,
  How I wonder what you are!
Up above the world so high,
Like a diamond in the sky.

When the blazing sun is gone,
When he nothing shines upon,
Then you show your little light,
Twinkle, twinkle, all the night.

When the traveller in the dark
Thanks you for your tiny spark:
How could he see where to go
If you did not twinkle so?

In the dark blue sky you keep,
Often through my curtains peep,
For you never shut your eye,
Till the sun is in the sky.

As your bright and tiny spark
Lights the traveller in the dark,
Though I know not what you are,
Twinkle, twinkle, little star.

WAS ever heard such noise and clamor!
  The hatchet's jealous of the hammer!

OH dear, what can the matter be
  Johnny's so long at the fair,
He promised to buy me a bunch of blue ribbons
  To tie up my bonny brown hair.

MAKE three-fourths of a cross,
  And a circle complete;
And let two semicircles
  On a perpendicular meet;
Next add a triangle
  That stands on two feet;
Next two semicircles,
  And a circle complete.
      [Tobacco.]

WHAT God never sees,
  What the King seldom sees,
What we see every day:
Read my riddle, I pray.
      [An equal.]

PURPLE, yellow, red, and green,
  The King cannot reach it, nor the
    Queen;
Nor can old Noll, whose power's so great:
Tell me this riddle while I count eight.
      [A rainbow.]

LADYBIRD, ladybird, fly away home!
  Your house is on fire, your children all
    gone,
All but one, and her name is Ann,
And she crept under the pudding pan.

THERE dwelt an old woman at Exeter;
  When visitors came it sore vexed her,
So for fear they should eat,
  She locked up all her meat,
This stingy old woman of Exeter.

THERE was a little girl who had a little curl
  Right in the middle of her forehead;
When she was good, she was very, very good,
And when she was bad she was horrid.

"LET us go to the woods," says Richard to Robin,
" Let us go to the woods,"says Robin to Bobbin,
" Let us go to the woods," says John all alone,
" Let us go to the woods," says every one.

" What to do there?" says Richard to Robin,
" What to do there?" says Robin to Bobbin,
" What to do there?" says John all alone,
" What to do there?" says every one.

" We will shoot a wren," says Richard to Robin,
" We will shoot a wren," says Robin to Bobbin,
" We will shoot a wren," says John all alone,
" We will shoot a wren," says every one.

" Then pounce, pounce," says Richard to Robin,
" Then pounce, pounce,"says Robin to Bobbin,
" Then pounce, pounce," says John all alone,
" Then pounce, pounce," says every one.

"She is dead, she is dead," says Richard to Robin,
"She is dead, she is dead," says Robin to Bobbin,
"She is dead, she is dead," says John all alone,
"She is dead, she is dead, says every one.

"How shall we get her home?" says Richard to Robin,
"How shall we get her home?" says Robin to Bobbin,
"How shall we get her home?" says John all alone,
"How shall we get her home?" says every one.

"In a cart with six horses," says Richard to Robin,
"In a cart with six horses," says Robin to Bobbin,
"In a cart with six horses," says John all alone,
"In a cart with six horses," says every one.

' How shall we get her dressed?" says Richard to Robin,
"How shall we get her dressed?" says Robin to Bobbin,
"How shall we get her dressed?" says John all alone,
"How shall we get her dressed?" says every one.

"We will hire seven cooks," says Richard to Robin,
"We will hire seven cooks," says Robin to Bobbin,
"We will hire seven cooks," says John all alone,
"We will hire seven cooks," says every one.

Little Miss Muffet sat on a tuffett, eating of curds and whey.

(Page 70)

Peter, Peter, pumpkin-eater, had a wife and couldn't keep

Rain, rain, go away, come again another day.

Little Bo-Peep has lost her sheep, and can't tell where to find th

TOM, Tom, the piper's son,
  Stole a pig and away he run;
The pig was eat, and Tom was beat,
And Tom ran crying down the street.

THERE was an old woman had three sons,
  Jerry, and James, and John:
Jerry was hung, James was drowned,
John was lost and never was found,
And there was an end of the three sons,
Jerry, and James, and John!

IF all the world were water,
  And all the water were ink,
What should we do for bread and cheese?
  What should we do for drink?

MASTER I have, and I am his man,
  Gallop a dreary dun;
Master I have, and I am his man,
And I'll get a wife as fast I can,
With a heighly, gayly, gamberally,
Higgledy, piggledy, niggledy, giggledy,
  Gallop a dreary dun.

A DOG and a cat went out together,
  To see some friends just out of town;
Said the cat to the dog,
"What d'ye think of the weather?"
"I think, ma'am, the rain will come down;
But don't be alarmed, for I've an umbrella
That will shelter us both," said this amiable
  fellow.

TOM he was a Piper's son,
  He learned to play when he was young;
But all the tune that he could play,
Was "Over the hills and far away."

Now, Tom with his pipe made such a noise,
That he pleased both the girls and the boys,
And they all stopped to hear him play,
"Over the hills and far away."

Tom with his pipe did play with such skill,
That those who heard him could never stand
    still;
Whenever they heard him they began to
    dance—
Even pigs on their hind legs would after him
    prance.

He met Old Dame Trot with a basket of eggs,
He used his pipe and she used her legs;
She danced about till the eggs were all broke;
She began to fret, but he laughed at the joke.

He saw a cross fellow was beating an ass,
Heavy laden with pots, pans, dishes, and glass;
He took out his pipe and played them a tune,
And the Jackass's load was lightened full soon.

EARLY to bed and early to rise
  Makes a man healthy, wealthy and wise.

[One child holds a wand to the face of another, repeating these lines, and making grimaces, to cause the latter to laugh, and so to the others; those who laugh paying a forfeit.]

BUFF says Buff to all his men,
  And I say Buff to you again;
Buff neither laughs nor smiles,
But carries his face
With a very good grace,
And passes the stick to the very next place!

POLLY put the kettle on,
  Polly put the kettle on,
Polly put the kettle on,
And let's drink tea.

Sukey take it off again,
Sukey take it off again,
Sukey take it off again,
They're all gone away.

FA, Fe, Fi, Fo, Fum!
  I smell the blood of an Englishman:
Be he alive, or be he dead,
I'll grind his bones to make me bread.

Polly put the kettle on, Polly put the kettle on, Polly put the kettle on, and let's drink tea.

(Page 60)

WEE Willie Winkie
    Runs through the town,
Up-stairs and down-stairs,
    In his night gown;
Rapping at the window,
    Crying at the lock,
"Are the children in their beds,
    For now it's ten o'clock?"

MOLLY, my sister, and I fell out,
    And what do you think it was all about?
She loved coffee and I loved tea,
And that was the reason we couldn't agree.

DAME Trot and her cat
    Led a peaceable life,
When they were not troubled
    With other folks' strife.

When Dame had her dinner
    Near Pussy would wait,
And was sure to receive
    A nice piece from her plate.

MISTER East gave a feast;
    Mister North laid the cloth;
Mister West did his best;
Mister South burnt his mouth
Eating cold potato.

UP hill spare me,
    Down hill 'ware me,
On level ground spare me not,
And in the stable forget me not.
        [A horse.]

RIDE, baby, ride,
  Pretty baby shall ride,
And have a little puppy-dog tied to her side,
And a little pussy-cat tied to her other,
And away she shall ride to see her grandmother,
  To see her grandmother,
  To see her grandmother.

BELL-HORSES, bell-horses,
  What time of day?
One o'clock, two o'clock,
  Off and away.

TWEEDLE-DUM and tweedle-dee
  Resolved to have a battle,
For tweedle-dum said tweedle-dee
  Had spoiled his nice new rattle.
Just then flew by a monstrous crow,
  As big as a tar-barrel,
Which frightened both the heroes so,
  They quite forgot their quarrel.

HEY, dorolot, dorolot!
  Hey, dorolay, dorolay!
Hey my bonny boat, bonny boat,
  Hey, drag away! drag away!

LITTLE Jack Jingle,
  He used to live single:
But when he got tired of this kind of life,
He left off being single; and live'd with his wife.

HUB a dub, dub,
  Three men in a tub;
The butcher, the baker,
The candlestick maker;
All jumped out of an Irish potato.

OLD Mistress McShuttle
  Lived in a coal-scuttle,
Along with her dog and her cat:
  What they ate I can't tell,
  But 'tis known very well
That none of the party were fat.

ONE, two, three,
  I love coffee,
And Billy loves tea.
How good you be!
One, two, three,
I love coffee,
And Billy loves tea.

THERE was a man who had no eyes,
　He went abroad to view the skies;
He saw a tree with apples on it,
He took no apples off, yet left no apples on it.
　　[The man had one eye, and the tree two apples upon it.]

BURNIE bee, burnie bee,
　Tell me when your wedding be?
If it be to-morrow day,
Take your wings and fly away.

THERE was and old woman of Harrow,
　Who visited in a wheelbarrow;
And her servant before,
Knocked loud at each door,
To announce the old woman of Harrow.

UP at Piccadilly, oh!
　The coachman takes his stand,
And when he meets a pretty girl
　He takes her by the hand;
Whip away forever, oh!
　Drive away so clever, oh!
All the way to Bristol, oh!
　He drives her four-in-hand.

OLD Grimes is dead, that good old man,
　We ne'er shall see him more;
He used to wear a long brown coat
All buttoned down before.

THERE was an Old Woman,
　And what do you think?
She lived upon nothing but
　Victuals and drink;
And though victuals and drink
　Were the chief of her diet,
This little Old Woman
　Could never be quiet.

THERE was a frog lived in a well,
  Kitty alone, Kitty alone;
There was a frog lived in a well;
  Kitty alone and I!

There was a frog lived in a well;
And a farce mouse in a mill,
Cock me carry, Kitty alone,
  Kitty alone and I.

This frog he would a-wooing ride,
  Kitty alone, Kitty alone;
This frog he would a-wooing ride,
And on a snail he got astride,
Cock me carry, Kitty alone,
  Kitty alone and I.

He rode till he came to my Lady Mouse Hall,
  Kitty alone, Kitty alone;
He rode till he came to my Lady Mouse Hall,
And there he did both knock and call,
Cock me carry, Kitty alone,
  Kitty alone and I.

Quoth he, " Miss Mouse, I'm come to thee,"—
Kitty alone, Kitty alone;
Quoth he, " Miss Mouse, I'm come to thee,
To see if thou canst fancy me."
Cock me carry, Kitty alone,
  Kitty alone and I.

Quoth she, " Answer I'll give you none"—
  Kitty alone, Kitty alone;
Quoth she, " Answer I'll give you none
Until my Uncle Rat come home."
Cock me carry, Kitty alone,
  Kitty alone and I.

" Sir, there's been a worthy gentleman "—
  Kitty alone, Kitty alone;
" Sir, there's been a worthy gentleman—
That's been here since you've been gone."
Cock me carry, Kitty alone,
  Kitty alone and I.

The frog he came whistling through the brook,
  Kitty alone, Kitty alone;
The frog he came whistling through the brook,
And there he met with a dainty duck.
Cock me carry, Kitty alone,
  Kitty alone and I.

This duck she swallowed him up with a pluck,
  Kitty alone, Kitty alone;
This duck she swallowed him up with a pluck,
So there's an end of my history-book.
Cock me carry, Kitty alone,
  Kitty alone and I.

WILLY, Willy Wilkin
    Kissed the maids a-milking, Fa, la, la!
And with his merry daffing
He set them all a-laughing, Ha, ha, ha!

HUSH-A-BYE, baby,
    Daddy is near;
Mamma is a lady,
And that's very clear.

JACK Spratt's pig,
    He was not very little,
Nor yet very big;
    He was not very lean,
He was not very fat—
    He'll do well for a grunt,
Says little Jack Spratt.

THERE was an owl lived in an oak,
    Wisky, wasky, weedle;
And every word he ever spoke
    Was fiddle, faddle, feedle.

A gunner chanced to come that way,
    Wisky, wasky, weedle;
Says he, "I'll shoot you, silly bird."
    Fiddle, faddle, feedle.

NANCY Dawson has grown so fine
    She won't get up to serve the swine;
She lies in bed till eight or nine,
So it's Oh, poor Nancy Dawson.

And do ye ken Nancy Dawson, honey?
The wife who sells the barley, honey?
She won't get up to feed her swine,
And do ye ken Nancy Dawson, honey?

YOUNG Roger came tapping at Dolly's
        window,
    Thumpaty, thumpaty, thump!
He asked for admittance, she answered him
        "No!"
    Frumpaty, frumpaty, frump!
"No, no, Roger, no! as you came you may
        go!"
    Stumpaty, stumpaty, stump!

A DUCK and a drake,
    And a halfpenny cake,
With a penny to pay the old baker.
    A hop and a scotch
    Is another notch,
Slitherum, slatherum, take her.

PUSSY-CAT ate the dumplings, the dump-
lings,
Pussy-cat ate the dumplings.
Mamma stood by, and cried, "Oh, fie!
Why did you eat the dumplings?"

GEORGEY Porgey, pudding and pie,
Kissed the girls and made them cry;
When the girls come out to play,
Georgey Porgey runs away.

WHAT'S the news of the day,
Good neighbor, I pray?
They say the balloon
Is gone up to the moon.

THE Man in the Moon looked out of the
moon,
Looked out of the moon and said,
"'Tis time for all children on the earth
To think about getting to bed!"

THERE was a little green house,
And in the little green house
There was a little brown house,
And in the little brown house
There was a little yellow house,
And in the little yellow house
There was a little white house,
And in the little white house
There was a little heart.
[A Walnut.]

LITTLE Miss Donnet
Wears a huge bonnet;
And hoops half as wide
As the mouth of the Clyde.

THERE was a little girl who wore a little
hood,
And a curl down the middle of her forehead;
When she was good, she was very, very good,
But when she was bad, she was horrid.

TEN little Injuns standing in a line—
    One went home, and then there were nine.

Nine little Injuns swinging on a gate—
One tumbled off, and then there were eight.

Eight little Injuns never heard of heaven—
One kicked the bucket, and then there were
    seven.

Seven little Injuns cutting up tricks—
One went to bed and then there were six.

Six little Injuns kicking all alive—
One broke his neck, and then there were five.

Five little Injuns on a cellar door—
One tumbled off, and then there were four.

Four little Injuns climbing up a tree—
One fell down, and then there were three.

Three little Injuns out in a canoe—
One fell overboard, and then there were two.

Two little Injuns fooling with a gun—
One shot the other, and then there was one.

One little Injun living all alone—
He got married, and then there was none!

THERE was an old woman of Gloucester,
    Whose parrot two guineas it cost her,
But its tongue never ceasing,
Was vastly displeasing
To the talkative woman of Gloucester.

THIS is the way the ladies ride,
    Tri, tre, tri, tree, tri, tre, tri, tree!
This is the way the ladies ride;
    Tri, tre, tri, tree, tri, tre, tri, tree!

This is the way the gentlemen ride!
        Gallop-a-trot, gallop-a-trot!
This is the way the gentlemen ride!
        Gallop-a-trot, gallop-a-trot!

This is the way the farmers ride!
        Hobbledy-hop, hobbledy-hop!
This is the way the farmers ride!
        Hobbledy-hop, hobbledy-hop!

DICKERY, dickery, dare,
    The pig flew up in the air;
The man in brown soon brought him
    down,
Dickery, dickery, dare.

FRIDAY night's dream, on Saturday told,
Is sure to come true, be it never so old.

SING a song of sixpence,
    A pocket full of rye;
Four-and-twenty blackbirds
    Baked in a pie.

When the pie was opened,
    The birds began to sing;
Was not that a dainty dish
    To set before the king?

The king was in his counting-house,
    Counting out his money;
The queen was in the parlor,
    Eating bread and honey.

The maid was in the garden,
    Hanging out the clothes;
Down came a blackbird,
    And pecked off her nose.

NIXIE, Dixie, hickory bow,
    Thirteen Dutchmen in a row;
Two corporals hold a piece of twine
    To help the Dutchmen form a line.

MY maid Mary she minds the dairy,
    While I go a-hoeing and mowing each
morn;
Gaily run the reel and the little spinning wheel,
    While I am singing and mowing my corn.

JERRY Hall, he is so small,
    A rat could eat him, hat and all.

LITTLE Jack Jelf
    Was put on the shelf
Because he could not spell " pie ";
    When his aunt, Mrs. Grace,
    Saw his sorrowful face,
She could not help saying, " Oh, fie !"

    And since Master Jelf
    Was put on the shelf
Because he could not spell "pie,"
    Let him stand there so grim,
    And no more about him,
For I wish him a very good-bye !

COME take up your hats, and away let us
   haste,
To the Butterfly's Ball, and the Grasshopper's
   Feast.
The trumpeter, Gad-fly, has summoned the crew,
And the revels are now only waiting for you.

On the smooth shaven grass, by the side of a
   wood,
Beneath a broad oak which for ages had stood,
See the children of earth, and the tenants of air,
To an evening's amusement together repair.

And there came the Beetle so blind and so black,
Who carried the Emmet, his friend, on his back,
And there came the Gnat and the Dragon-fly
   too,
With all their relations, green, orange, and blue.

And there came the Moth, with her plumage
   of down,
And the Hornet with jacket of yellow and
   brown;
And with him the Wasp, his companion, did
   bring,
But they promised that evening to lay by their
   sting.

Then the sly little Dormouse peeped out of
   his hole,
And led to the Feast his blind cousin the Mole:
And the Snail, with her horns peeping out of
   her shell,
Came, fatigued with the distance, the length of
   an ell.

A mushroom the table, and on it was spread
A water-dock leaf, which their table-cloth made.
The viands were various, to each of their taste.
And the Bee brought the honey to sweeten the
   feast.

With steps most majestic the Snail did advance,
And he promised the gazers a minuet to dance;
But they all laughed so loud that he drew in
   his head,
And went in his own little chamber to bed.

Then, as evening gave way to the shadows of
   night,
Their watchman, the Glow-worm, came out
   with his light.
So home let us hasten, while yet we can see,
For no watchman is waiting for you or for
   me.

LITTLE Miss Muffet
    Sat on a tuffet,
Eating of curds and whey;
    There came a spider,
    And sat down beside her,
And frightened Miss Muffet away.

TWO monkeys came from their native wood,
    To view the haunts and ways of men;
Two mortal hours they silent stood,
    And then, content, went back again.

A WHALE, I am told, swallowed Jonah of
    old,
    And kept him three days in his belly;
I should think such a squeeze would have
    made Jonah sneeze,
    And mashed him all up to a jelly.

WHEN the wind is in the east,
    'Tis neither good for man nor beast.
When the wind is in the north,
The skilful fisher goes not forth.
When the wind is in the south,
It blows the bait in the fishers' mouth.
When the wind is in the west,
Then 'tis at the very best.

THERE was an old woman in Surrey,
    Who was morn, noon, and night in a
        hurry;
Called her husband a fool,
Drove the children to school,
The worrying old woman of Surrey.

I HAD a little hen, the prettiest ever seen,
    She washed me the dishes, and kept the
        house clean.
She went to the mill to fetch me some flour,
She brought it home in less than an hour;
She baked me my bread, she brewed me my
    ale,
She sat by the fire, and told many a fine tale.

LITTLE Robin Red-breast
    Sat upon a rail,
Needle, naddle, went his head,
    Wiggle, waggle, went his tail.

THERE was a little woman, as I've been told,
    Who was not very young, nor yet very old;
Now this little woman her living got
By selling codlins, hot, hot, hot!

A was an angler,
　　Went out in a fog;
Who fish'd all the day,
　　And caught only a frog.

B was cook Betty,
　　A-baking a pie
With ten or twelve apples
　　All piled up on high.

C was a custard
　　In a glass dish,
With as much cinnamon
　　As you could wish.

D was fat Dick,
　　Who did nothing but eat;
He would leave book and play
　　For a nice bit of meat.

E was an egg,
　　In a basket with more,
Which Peggy will sell
　　For a shilling a score.

F was a fox,
　　So cunning and sly:
Who looks at the hen-roost—
　　I need not say why.

G was a greyhound,
　　As fleet as the wind;
In the race or the course
　　Left all others behind.

H was a heron,
　　Who lived near a pond;
Of gobbling the fishes
　　He was wondrously fond.

I was the ice
　　On which Billy would skate;
So up went his heels,
　　And down went his pate.

J was Joe Jenkins,
　　Who played on the fiddle;
He began twenty tunes,
　　But left off in the middle.

K was a kitten,
　　Who jumped at a cork,
And learned to eat mice
　　Without plate, knife, or fork.

L was a lark,
　　Who sings us a song,
And wakes us betimes
　　Lest we sleep too long.

M was Miss Molly,
　Who turned in her toes,
And hung down her head
　Till her knees touched her nose.

N was a nosegay,
　Sprinkled with dew,
Pulled in the morning
　And presented to you.

O was an owl,
　Who looked wondrously wise;
But he's watching a mouse
　With his large round eyes.

P was a parrot,
　With feathers like gold,
Who talks just as much,
　And no more than he's told.

Q is the Queen
　Who governs the land,
And sits on a throne
　Very lofty and grand.

R is a raven
　Perched on an oak,
Who with a gruff voice
　Cries croak, croak, croak!

S was a stork
　With a very long bill,
Who swallows down fishes
　And frogs to his fill.

T is a trumpeter
　Blowing his horn,
Who tells us the news
　As we rise in the morn.

U is a unicorn,
　Who, as it is said,
Wears an ivory bodkin
　On his forehead.

V is a vulture
  Who eats a great deal,
Devouring a dog
  Or a cat as a meal.

W was a watchman
  Who guarded the street,
Lest robbers or thieves
  The good people should meet.

X was King Xerxes,
  Who, if you don't know,
Reigned over Persia
  A great while ago.

Y is the year
  That is passing away,
And still growing shorter
  Every day.

Z is a zebra,
  Whom you've heard of before;
So here ends my rhyme
  Till I find you some more.

THERE was a man in our town,
  He couldn't pay his rent;
And so one lovely moonlight night,
  To another town he went.

FATHER, may I go to war?
  Yes, you may, my son;
Wear your woollen comforter,
  But don't fire off your gun.

O, THE grand old Duke of York,
  He had ten thousand men;
He marched them up a great big hill,
  And he marched them down again!
So when they were up, they were up,
  And when they were down, they were down;
And when they were neither down nor up,
  They were neither up nor down.

HIGH, diddle doubt, my candle's out!
　　My little maid is not at home;
Saddle my hog and bridle my dog,
　　And fetch my little maid home.

LADY-BUG, lady-bug,
　　Fly away home,
Your house is on fire,
　　Your children will burn.

DONKEY, donkey, old and gray,
　　Ope your mouth, and gently bray;
Lift your ears and blow your horn,
To wake the world this sleepy morn.

THERE was an old woman of Leeds,
　　Who spent all her time in good deeds;
She worked for the poor
Till her fingers were sore,
This pious old woman of Leeds!

BESSY Bell and Mary Gray,
　　They were two bonny lasses,
They built their house upon the lea,
　　And covered it with rushes.

Bessy kept the garden gate,
　　And Mary kept the pantry;
Bessy always had to wait,
　　While Mary lived in plenty.

POLLY put the kettle on,
　　Susy took it off;
Aunt Jemima's little girl,
　　Has got the whooping cough.

HINK minx! the old witch winks,
　　The fat begins to fry:
There's nobody home but jumping Joan,
　　Father, Mother, and I,

THERE was a Piper had a cow,
  And he had naught to give her,
He pull'd out his pipes and play'd her a tune,
  And bade the cow consider.

The cow considered very well,
  And gave the Piper a penny,
And bade him play the other tune,
  "Corn rigs are bonny."

TWO legs sat upon three legs,
  With one leg is his lap;
In comes four legs,
And runs away with one leg;
Up jumps two legs,
Catches up three legs,
Throws if after four legs,
And makes him bring one leg back.
  [A man, a leg of lamb, a dog, and a three-legged stool.]

PUSSY sits beside the fire. How can she be
  fair?
In walks a little doggy—Pussy, are you there?
So, so, Mistress Pussy, how do you do?
Thank you, thank you, little dog,
I'm very well just now.

[This is said to be a certain cure for the hiccough if repeated in one breath.]

WHEN a twister a-twisting, will twist him
  a twist,
For the twisting of his twist, he three times
  doth intwist;
But if one of the twines of the twist do un-
  twist,
The twine that untwisteth, untwisteth the twist.
Untwirling the twine that untwisteth between,
He twirls, with the twister, the two in a twine
Then twice having twisted the twines of the
  twine,
He twisteth the twine he had twined in twain.
The twain that, in twining, before in the twine,
As twines were intwisted, he now doth untwine;
'Twixt the twain intertwisting a twine more
  between,
He, twirling his twister, makes a twist of the
  twine.

OVER the water,
  And under the water,
And always with its head down.
  [Icicle.]

THREE straws on a staff
  Would make a baby cry and laugh.

COME hither, little puppy dog;
  I'll give you a new collar,
If you will learn to read your book
  And be a clever scholar,
No, no! replied the puppy dog,
  I've other fish to fry,
For I must learn to guard your house,
  And bark when thieves come nigh.
With a tingle, tangle, tit-mouse!
  Robin knows great A,
And B, and C, and D, and E, F, G,
  H, I, J, K.

Come hither, little pussy cat;
  If you'll your grammar study
I'll give you silver clogs to wear,
  Whene'er the gutter's muddy.
No! whilst I grammar learn, says Puss,
  Your house will in a trice
Be overrun from top to bottom
  With flocks of rats and mice.
With a tingle, tangle, tit-mouse!
  Robin knows great A,
And B, and C, and D, and E, F, G,
  H, I, J, K.

Come hither, pretty cockatoo;
  Come and learn your letters,
And you shall have a knife and fork
  To eat with, like your betters,
No, no! the cockatoo replied,
  My beak will do as well;
I'd rather eat my victuals thus
  Than go and learn to spell.
With a tingle, tangle, tit-mouse!
  Robin knows great A,
And B, and C, and D, and E, F, G,
  H, I, J, K.

Come hither, then, good little boy,
  And learn your alphabet,
And you a pair of boots and spurs,
  Like your papa's, shall get.
Oh, yes! I'll learn my alphabet;
  And when I well can read,
Perhaps papa will give, me, too,
  A pretty long-tail'd steed.
With a tingle, tangle, tit-mouse!
  Robin knows great A,
And B, and C, and D, and E, F, G,
  H, I, J, K.

WHERE have you been all the day,
          My boy, Willy?
Where have you been all the day,
          My boy, Willy?
  "I've been all the day
Courting of a lady gay;
But oh! she's too young
To be taken from her mammy."

What work can she do,
          My boy, Willy?
Can she bake and can she brew,
          My boy, Willy?
  "She can brew and she can bake,
And she can make our wedding-cake;
But oh! she's too young
To be taken from her mammy."

What age may she be,
          My boy, Willy?
What age may she be,
          My boy, Willy?
  "Twice two, twice seven,
Twice ten, twice eleven;
But oh! she's too young
To be taken from her mammy."

QUIXOTE Quicksight, quiz'd a queerish
    quidbox,
A queerish quidbox Quixote Quicksight
    quiz'd;
If Quixote Quicksight quiz'd a queerish quid-
    box,
Wheres the queerish quidbox Quixote Quick-
    sight quiz'd?

THOMAS A' Tattamus took two Ts,
    To tie two tups to two tall trees,
To frighten the terrible Thomas A' Tattamus!
Tell me how many Ts there are in *that*.

WASH me, and comb me,
    And lay me down softly,
And set me on a bank to dry;
That I may look pretty
When some one comes by.

WE'RE all jolly boys, and we're coming
    with a noise,
Our stockings shall be made
Of the finest silk,
And our tails shall trail the ground.

"WHERE are you going, my pretty maid?"
　　"I'm going a-milking, sir," she said.

"May I go with you, my pretty maid?"
"You're kindly welcome, sir," she said.

"What is your father, my pretty maid?"
"My father's a farmer, sir," she said.

"Say, will you marry me, my pretty maid?"
"Yes, if you please, kind sir," she said.

"What is your fortune, my pretty maid?"
"My face is my fortune, sir," she said.

"Then I can't marry you, my pretty maid."
"Nobody asked you, sir!" she said.

IF wishes were horses, beggars would ride.
　　If turnips were watches, I would wear one
　　　by my side,
And if "ifs" and "ands" were pots and pans,
There'd be no work for tinkers!

WHAT is the rhyme for porringer?
　　The King he had a daughter fair,
And gave the Prince of Orange her.

CLAP, clap handies,
　　Mammie's wee, wee ain;
　Clap, clap handies,
Daddie's comin' hame,
Hame till his bonny wee bit laddie;
　Clap, clap handies,
　My wee, wee ain.

COME, my dear children,
　　Up is the sun,
Birds are all singing,
　And morn has begun.

Up from the bed, Miss,
　Out on the lea;
The horses are waiting
　For you and for me!

THE dove says, "Coo, coo, what shall I do?
  I can scarce maintain two."
"Pooh! pooh!" says the wren; "I have got ten,
And keep them all like gentlemen."

PIT, pat, well-a-day,
  Little Robin flew away;
Where can little Robin be?—
Gone into the cherry-tree.

PLEASE to remember
  The Fifth of November,
Gunpowder, treason, and plot;
I know no reason
  Why gunpowder treason
Should ever be forgot.

POOR Dog Bright
  Ran off with all his might,
Because the cat was after him—
Poor Dog Bright!

Poor Cat Fright
Ran off with all her might,
Because the dog was after her—
Poor cat Fright!

PUSSY-CAT, wussy-cat, with a white foot,
  When is your wedding? for I'll come to't.
The beer's to brew, the bread's to bake,
Pussy-cat, pussy-cat, don't be too late.

"ROBERT Barnes, fellow fine,
  Can you shoe this horse of mine?"
"Yes, good sir, that I can,
As well as any other man:
Here a nail, and there a prod,
And now, good sir, your horse is shod."

THE cuckoo's a fine bird,
  He sings as he flies;
He brings us good tidings,
  He tells us no lies.

He sucks little birds' eggs,
  To make his voice clear;
And when he sings "cuckoo!"
  The summer is near.

SMILING girls, rosy boys,
  Come and buy my little toys;
Monkeys made of gingerbread,
And sugar horses painted red.

PETER, Peter, pumpkin-eater;
    Had a wife, and couldn't keep her;
He put her in a pumpkin shell,
And there he kept her very well.

Peter, Peter, pumpkin-eater;
Had another and didn't love her;
Peter learned to read and spell,
And then he loved her very well.

TOMMY kept a chandler's shop,
    Richard went to buy a mop;
Tommy gave him such a knock,
That sent him him out of his chandler's shop.

MY pussy cat
    Has got the gout,
And the rats and mice
Can play about.

DOODLE doodle doo,
    The Princess lost her shoe:
Her Highness hopped,—
The fiddler stopped,
Not knowing what to do.

BARBER, barber, shave a pig;
    How many hairs will make a wig?
"Four and twenty, that's enough,"
Give the poor barber a pinch of snuff.

[To be read rapidly.]

PETER Piper picked a peck
    Of pickled pepper;
A peck of pickled pepper
    Peter Piper picked;
If Peter Piper picked a peck
    Of pickled pepper,
Where's the peck of pickled pepper
    Peter Piper picked?

THERE was an old man of Tobago,
    Who lived on rice, gruel, and sago,
        Till, much to his bliss,
        His physician said this,
To a leg, sir, of mutton you may go.

LEG over leg,
    As the dog went to Dover,
When he came to a stile,
    Jump he went over.

DIDDLEDY, diddledy, dumpty;
  The cat ran up the plum-tree.
I'll lay you a crown
I'll fetch you down;
So diddledy, diddledy, dumpty.

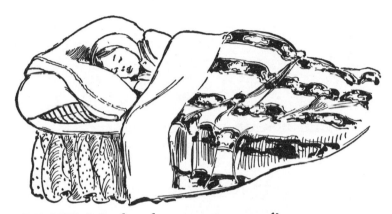

ELSIE Marley has grown so fine,
  She won't get up to serve the swine;
But lies in bed till eight or nine,
And surely she does take her time.

BROW brinky,
  Eye winky,
Chin choppy,
  Nose noppy,
    Cheek cherry,
      Mouth merry.

MERRY are the bells, and merry would
    they ring,
Merry was myself, and merry could I sing;
With a merry ding-dong, happy, gay, and free,
And a merry sing-song, happy let us be!

Waddle goes your gait, and hollow are your
    hose,
Noodle goes your pate, and purple is your
    nose;
Merry is your sing-song, happy, gay, and free,
With a merry ding-dong, happy let us be!

Merry have we met, and merry have we been,
Merry let us part, and merry meet again;
With our merry sing-song, happy, gay, and free,
And a merry ding-dong, happy let us be!

BYE, baby, bunting,
  Daddy's gone a-hunting,
To get a little rabbit skin
To wrap his baby bunting in.

CHARLEY loves good cake and ale,
  Charley loves good candy,
Charley loves to kiss the girls,
  When they are clean and handy.

THE Dog will come when he is called,
  The Cat will walk away;
The Monkey's cheek is very bald;
  The Goat is fond of play.
The Parrot is a prate-apace,
  He knows not what he says:
The noble Horse will win the race,
  Or draw you in a chaise.

The Sparrow steals the cherry ripe,
  The Elephant is wise,
The Blackbird charms you with his pipe,
  The false Hyena cries,
The Hen guards well her little chicks,
  The Cow her hoof is slit,
The Beaver builds with mud and sticks,
  The Lapwing cries "Peewit."

GOD bless the master of this house,
  The mistress bless also,
And all the little children
  That round the table go;
And all your kin and kinsmen,
  That dwell both far and near:
I wish you a merry Christmas,
  And a happy new year.

"FIRE! fire! said the town crier;
  "Where? where?" said Goody Blair;
"Down the town," said Goody Brown;
"I'll go and see't," said Goody Fleet;
"So will I," said Goody Fry.

COME hither, sweet robin,
  And be not afraid,
I would not hurt even a feather;
Come hither, sweet Robin,
  And pick up some bread,
To feed you this very cold weather.

I don't mean to frighten you,
    Poor little thing,
  And pussy-cat is not behind me;
So hop about pretty,
    And drop down your wing,
  And pick up some crumbs,
    And don't mind me.

HERE we go up, up, up,
  Here we go down, down, downy,
And here we go backwards and forwards,
And here we go round, round, roundy.

LITTLE Tom Twig bought a fine bow and
arrow,
And what did he shoot? why, a poor little
sparrow,
Oh, fie, little Tom, with your fine bow and
arrow,
How cruel to shoot at a poor little sparrow.

MONDAY alone,
Tuesday together,
Wednesday we walk
When it's fine weather.
Thursday we kiss,
Friday we cry,
Saturday's hours
Seem almost to fly.
But of all the days in the week
We will call
Sunday, the rest day,
The best day of all.

DING, dong, darrow,
The cat and the sparrow;
The little dog has burnt his tail,
And he shall be hanged to-morrow.

WHEN Jacky's a very good boy,
He shall have cakes and a custard;
But when he does nothing but cry,
He shall have nothing but mustard.

IN a cottage in Fife
Lived a man and his wife,
Who, believe me were comical folk;
For two people's surprise,
They both saw with their eyes,
And their tongues moved whenever they spoke!

When quite fast asleep,
I've been told that, to keep
There eyes open they scarce could contrive:
They walked on their feet,
And 'twas thought what they eat
Helped, with drinking, to keep them alive!

I LOVE you well, my little brother,
And you are fond of me;
Let us be kind to one another,
As brothers ought to be.
You shall learn to play with me,
And learn to use my toys;
And then I think that we shall be
Two happy little boys.

DOGS in the garden, catch 'em, Towser;
  Cows in the cornfield, run, boys, run;
Cats in the cream-pot, run, girls, run, girls;
  Fire on the mountains, run, boys, run.

AS I was going up Pippen Hill,
  Pippen Hill was dirty;
There I met a pretty Miss,
  And she dropped me a curtsy.

Little Miss, pretty Miss,
  Blessing light upon you;
If I had half a crown a-day,
  I'd spend it all upon you.

DOCTOR Faustus was a good man,
  He whipped his scholars now and then;
When he whipped them he made them dance
Out of Scotland into France,
Out of France into Spain,
And then he whipped them back again!

BOW-WOW, says the dog;
  Mew, mew, says the cat;
Grunt, grunt, goes the hog;
  And squeak goes the rat.

Tu-whu, says the owl;
  Caw, caw, says the crow;
Quack, quack, says the duck;
  And what sparrows say you know.

So, with sparrows, and owls,
  With rats, and with dogs,
With ducks, and with crows,
  With cats, and with hogs.

A fine song I have made,
  To please you, my dear;
And if it's well sung,
  'Twill be charming to hear.

ONE old Oxford ox opening oysters;
  Two tee-totums totally tired of trying to
    trot to Tadbury;
Three tall tigers tippling tenpenny tea;
Four fat friars fanning fainting flies;
Five frippy Frenchmen foolishly fishing for
    flies;
Six sportmen shooting snipes;
Seven Severn salmons swallowing shrimps;
Eight Englishmen eagerly examining Europe;
Nine nimble noblemen nibbling nonpareils;
Ten tinkers tinkling upon ten tin tinder-boxes
    with tenpenny tacks;
Eleven elephants elegantly equipped;
Twelve typographical topographers typically
    translating typcs.

HIGH diddle ding,
  Did you hear the bells ring?
The Parliament soldiers are gone to the
    King;
Some they did laugh, some they did cry,
To see the Parliament soldiers pass by.

WEAR you a hat, or wear you a crown,
  All that goes up must surely come down.

HERE we go round the mulberry bush,
  The mulberry bush, the mulberry bush,
Here we go round the mulberry bush,
On a cold and frosty morning.

This is the way we wash our hands,
Wash our hands, wash our hands,
This is the way we wash our hands,
On a cold and frosty morning.

This is the way we wash our clothes,
Wash our clothes, wash our clothes,
This is the way we wash our clothes,
On a cold and frosty morning.

This is the way we go to school,
Go to school, go to school,
This is the way we go to school,
On a cold and frosty morning.

This is the way we come out of school,
Come out of school, come out of school,
This is the way we come out of school,
On a cold and frosty morning.

THE calf, the goose, the bee,
  The world is ruled by these three.
[Parchment, pens, and wax.]

BIRDS of a feather flock together,
  And so will pigs and swine;
Rats and mice will have their choice,
  And so will I have mine.

LITTLE boy blue, come blow your horn;
  The Sheep's in the meadow, the cow's in
    the corn.
Where's the little boy that looks after the sheep?
He's under the hay-cock, fast a-sleep.
Will you wake him?   No, not I;
For if I do, he'll be sure to cry.

SPEAK when you're spoken to,
  Come when once called;
Shut the door after you,
  And turn to the wall!

CHRISTMAS comes but once a year,
  And when it comes it brings good cheer.

A CARRION crow sat on an oak,
  Fol de riddle, lol de riddle, he ding do,
Watching a tailor shape his coat!
  Sing he, sing ho, the old carrion crow,
  Fol de riddle, lol de riddle, he ding do.

Wife, bring me my old bent bow,
  Fol de riddle, lol de riddle, he ding do,
That I may shoot you carrion crow.
  Sing he, sing ho, the old carrion crow.
  Fol de riddle, lol de riddle, he ding do.

The tailor shot, and he missed his mark,
  Fol de riddle, lol de riddle, he ding do,
And shot the miller's sow right through the
    heart.
  Sing he, sing ho, the old carrion crow.
  Fol de riddle, lol de riddle, he ding do.

Wife! oh wife! bring brandy in a spoon,
  Fol de riddle, lol de riddle, he ding do.
For the old miller's sow is in a swoon,
  Sing he, sing ho, the old carrion crow,
  Fol de riddle, lol de riddle, he ding do.

A SUNSHINY shower
  Won't last half an hour.

I HAVE a little sister; they call her Peep, Peep.
She wades the water deep, deep, deep;
She climbs the mountains, high, high, high—
Poor little thing! she has but one eye.

[A Star.]

OVER the water, and over the sea,
    And over the water to Charley;
Charley loves good ale and wine,
And Charley loves good brandy,
And Charley loves a pretty girl,
As sweet as sugar candy.

Over the water, and over the sea,
And over the water to Charley;
I'll have none of your nasty beef,
Nor I'll have none of your barley;
But I'll have some of your very best flour,
To make a white cake for my Charley.

I'LL sing you a song,
    Though not very long,
Yet I think it as pretty as any;
Put your hand in your purse,
You'll never be worse,
And give the poor singer a penny.

UP by the chimney there is a small man,
    Who holds in his hands a stick and a fan;
When the winds rage he strikes a fierce blow,
And thus their direction tells mortals below.

AS little Jennie Wren
    Was sitting by the shed,
She waggled with her tail,
    And nodded with her head.
She waggled with her tail,
    And nodded with her head,
As little Jennie Wren
    Was sitting by the shed.

OH, the little rusty, dusty, rusty miller!
    I'll not change my wife for either gold or siller.

MY grandmother sent me a new-fashioned
    three-cornered cambric country-cut
handkerchief. Not an old-fashioned three-
cornered cambric country-cut handkerchief,
but a new-fashioned three-cornered cambric
country-cut handkerchief.

A FAMOUS old woman was Madam
McBright,
She slept all day, and slept all night;
One hour was given to victuals and drink,
And only a minute was taken to think.

L ITTLE Nancy Etticote,
In a white petticoat,
With a red nose;
The longer she stands,
The shorter she grows.
[A Candle.]

A S I went through the garden gap,
Who should I meet but Dick Red-cap!
A stick in his hand, a stone in his throat,
If you'll tell me this riddle, I'll give you a groat.
[A Cherry.]

T HE fair maid who, the first of May,
Goes to the fields at break of day,
And washes in dew from the hawthorn tree,
Will ever after handsome be.

H OT cross buns,
Hot cross buns,
One a penny, two a penny,
Hot cross buns.
If your daughters
Don't like 'em,
Give them to your sons,
One a penny, two a penny,
Hot cross buns.

R OBIN the Bobbin, the big-bellied Ben,
He eat more meat than fourscore men;
He eat a cow, he eat a calf,
He eat a hog and a half;
He eat a church, he eat a steeple,
He eat the priest and all the people!
A cow and a calf,
An ox and a half,
A church and a steeple,
And all the good people,
And yet he complain'd that his stomach
wasn't full.

Hot cross buns, hot cross buns, One a penny, two a penny, hot cross buns.

(Page 88)

LONDON Bridge is broken down,
  Dance o'er my Lady Lee;
London Bridge is broken down,
  With a gay lady.

How shall we build it up again?
  Dance o'er my Lady Lee;
How shall we build it up again?
  With a gay lady.

Build it up with silver and gold,
  Dance o'er my Lady Lee;
Build it up with silver and gold,
  With a gay lady.

Silver and gold will be stole away,
  Dance o'er my Lady Lee;
Silver and gold will be stole away,
  With a gay lady.

Build it up with iron and steel,
  Dance o'er my Lady Lee;
Build it up with iron and steel,
  With a gay lady.

Iron and steel will bend and bow,
  Dance o'er my Lady Lee;
Iron and steel will bend and bow,
  With a gay lady.

Build it up with wood and clay,
  Dance o'er my Lady Lee;
Build it up with wood and clay,
  With a gay lady.

Wood and clay will wash away,
  Dance o'er my Lady Lee;
Wood and clay will wash away,
  With a gay lady.

Build it up with stone so strong,
  Dance o'er my Lady Lee;
Huzza! 'twill last for ages long,
  With a gay lady.

MONDAY'S bairn is fair of face,
  Tuesday's bairn is full of grace,
Wednesday's bairn is full of woe,
Thursday's bairn has far to go,
Friday's bairn is loving and giving,
Saturday's bairn works hard for its living;
But the bairn that is born on the Sabbath day
Is bonny, and blithe, and good and gay.

OH, dear! what can the matter be?
  Two old women got up an apple-tree;
One came down,
And the other stayed till Saturday.

THERE was an idle boy,
    And he rode a little calf called Spotty.
Now that tells my story half:

But the calf kicked up his heels,
    And rolled him in the fields.
And that tells my story all, little Totty.

HERE am I, little jumping Joan,
    When nobody's with me, I'm always
alone.

THERE was a rat, for want of stairs,
    Went down a rope to say his prayers.

O MOTHER, I shall be married
    To Mr. Punchinello,
  To Mr. Punch,
    To Mr. Joe,
      To Mr. Nell,
        To Mr. Lo,
          To Mr. Punch, Mr. Joe,
            Mr. Nell, Mr. Lo,
              Mr. Punchinello.

[Game on a child's features.]

HERE sits the Lord Mayor   .   *forehead.*
        Here sit his two men   .   .   *eyes.*
Here sits the cock   .   .   .   .   *right cheek.*
    Here sits the hen   .   .   .   .   *left cheek.*
Here sit the little chickens   .   .   *top of nose.*
    Here they run in   .   .   .   .   *mouth.*
Chinchopper, chinchopper,
    Chinchopper, chin!   .   .   .   *chuck the chin.*

[Say quick.]

IN fir tar is.
    In oak none is.
In mud eel is.
In clay none is.
Goat eat ivy.
Mare eat oats.

NOAH of old did build an Ark,
　Loddy, shoddy, whack fi oddy, ki a.
Noah of old did build an Ark
Of spicy Gopher-wood and bark,
To float above the deluge dark.
　Cho.—Loddy, shoddy, whack fi oddy, ki a.

Now on this Ark they had no sails,
　Loddy, shoddy, whack fi oddy, ki a.
Now on this Ark they had no sails.
For it was made—(and true the tail)
Without a mast to breast the gale.
　Cho.—Loddy, shoddy, whack fi oddy, ki a.

He built it high, he built it strong,
　Loddy, shoddy, whack fi oddy, ki a.
He built it high, he built it strong,
He built it wide, he built it long,
To hold a jolly, motley throng.
　Cho.—Loddy, shoddy, whack fi oddy, ki a.

There were the Elephant and Bee,
　Loddy, shoddy, whack fi oddy, ki a.
There were the Elephant and Bee,
The Hippopotamus and Flea,
The Giraffe and Chick-a-dee-dee.
　Cho.—Loddy, shoddy, whack fi oddy, ki a.

The Cock-a-doodle and the Ass,
　Loddy, shoddy, whack fi oddy, ki a.
The Cock-a-doodle and the Ass,
And three young men, each with his lass,
Shem, Ham, and Japhet had a pass!
　Cho.—Loddy, shoddy, whack fi oddy, ki a.

Noah of old, and Noah's dame,
　Loddy, shoddy, whack fi oddy, ki a.
Noah of old, and Noah's dame,
I think I never heard her name,
But she went in tho' all the same.
　Cho.—Loddy, shoddy, whack fi oddy, ki a.

But best of all, my little dears,
　Loddy, shoddy, whack fi oddy, ki a.
But best of all, my little dears,
'T will most delight your list'ning ears,
So give with me three hearty cheers.
　Cho.—Loddy, shoddy, whack fi oddy, ki a.

To hear that sheltered by that truce,
　Loddy, shoddy, whack fi oddy, ki a.
To hear that sheltered by that truce,
Loved more than Monkey, Owl, or Moose,
In walked *your precious* Mother Goose!
　Cho.—Quack, quack, loddy sis quack whack
　　fi oddy, ki a. *Repeat.*

ONE, two, buckle my shoe;
    Three, four, shut the door;
Five, six, pick up sticks;
Seven, eight, lay them straight;
Nine, ten, a good fat hen;
Eleven, twelve, who will delve;
Thirteen, fourteen, maid's a-courting;
Fifteen, sixteen, maids a-kissing;
Seventeen, eighteen, maids a-waiting;
Nineteen, twenty, my stomach's empty.

HIGHER than a house, higher than a tree,
    Oh, whatever can it be?
        [A Star.]

HERE comes a poor woman from baby
    land,
With five small children on her hand:
One can brew, the other can bake,
The other can make a pretty round cake,
One can sit in the garden and spin,
Another can make a fine bed for the king:
Pray, ma'am, will you take one in!

FORMED long ago, yet made to-day
    Employed while others sleep;
What few would like to give away,
    Nor any wish to keep.
        [A Bed.]

ROBERT Rowley rolled a round roll
    round,
A round roll Robert Rowley rolled round;
    Where rolled the round roll
    Robert Rowley rolled round?

THERE was a man rode through our
    Gray Grizzle was his name;   [town,
His saddle-bow was gilt with gold,
    Three times I've named his name.

A FOR the Ape, that we saw at the fair;

B for the Blockhead, who ne'er shall go there;

C for a Cauliflower, white as a curd;

D for a Duck, a very good bird;

E for an Egg, good in pudding or pies;

F for a Farmer, rich, honest and wise;

G for a Gentleman, void of all care;

H for the Hound, that ran down the hare;

I for an Indian, sooty and dark;

K for the Keeper, that looked to the park;

L for a Lark, that soared in the air;

M for a Mole, that ne'er could get there;

N for Sir Nobody, ever in fault;

O for an Otter, that ne'er could be caught;

P for a Pudding, stuck full of plums;

Q was for Quartering it—see, here he comes;

R for a Rook, that croaked in the trees;

S for a Sailor, that ploughed the deep seas;

T for a top, that doth prettily spin;

V for a Virgin, of delicate mein;

W for Wealth, in gold, silver, and pence;

X for old Xenophon, noted for sense;

Y for the Yew, which forever is green;

Z for the Zebra, that belongs to the Queen.

A GLASS of milk and a slice of bread,
And then good-night, we must go to bed.

IT costs little Gossip her income for shoes,
To travel about and carry the news.

LITTLE Jack Dandy-prat was my first suitor;
  He had a dish and a spoon, and he'd some
    pewter;
He'd linen and woollen, and woollen and linen,
A little pig in a string cost him five shilling.

LITTLE girl, little girl, where have you been?
  Gathering roses to give to the queen.
Little girl, little girl, what gave she you?
She gave me a diamond as big as my shoe.

DAFFY-DOWN-DILLY has come
      up to town,
In a fine petticoat and a green gown.

"CROAK!" said the toad, "I'm hungry, I
      think;
To-day I've had nothing to eat or to drink.
I'll crawl to a garden and jump through the
      pales,
  And there I'll dine nicely on slugs and on
    snails."

"Ho, ho!" quoth the frog, "is that what you
      mean?
Then I'll hop away to the next meadow stream;
There I will drink, and eat worms and slugs too,
And then I shall have a good dinner like you."

THERE was a man in our town,
      And he was wondrous wise;
He jumped into a bramble bush,
  And scratch'd out both his eyes;

And when he saw his eyes were out,
  With all his might and main,
He jump'd into another bush,
  And scratch'd them in again.

THERE was a little one-eyed gunner,
  Who kill'd all the birds that died last
    summer.

THIS is the House that Jack built.
This is the Malt
That lay in the house that Jack built.

This is the Rat, that ate the malt,
That lay in the house that Jack built.

This is the Cat, that killed the rat,
That ate the malt,
That lay in the house that Jack built.

This is the Dog, that worried the cat,
That killed the rat, that ate the malt,
That lay in the house that Jack built.

This is the Cow, with the crumpled horn
That tossed the dog, that worried the cat,
That killed the rat, that ate the malt,
That lay in the house that Jack built.

This is the Maiden all forlorn,
That milk'd the cow with the crumpled horn,
That toss'd the dog, that worried the cat,
That kill'd the rat, that ate the malt,
That lay in the house that Jack built.

This is the Man all tatter'd and torn,
That kiss'd the maiden all forlorn,
That milked the cow with the crumpled horn,
That toss'd the dog, that worried the cat,
That kill'd the rat, that ate the malt,
That lay in the house that Jack built.

This is the Priest all shaven and shorn,
That married the man all tatter'd and torn,
That kiss'd the maiden all forlorn,
That milk'd the cow with the crumpled horn,
That toss'd the dog, that worried the cat,
That kill'd the rat, that ate the malt,
That lay in the house that Jack built.

This is the Cock that crow'd in the morn,
That waked the priest all shaven and shorn,

That married the man all tatter'd and torn,
That kiss'd the maiden all forlorn,
That milk'd the cow with the crumpled horn,
That toss'd the dog, that worried the cat,
That kill'd the rat, that ate the malt,
That lay in the house that Jack built.

This is the Farmer who sow'd the corn,
That kept the cock that crow'd in the morn,
That waked the priest all shaven and shorn,
That married the man all tatter'd and torn,
That kiss'd the maiden all forlorn,
That milk'd the cow with the crumpled horn,
That toss'd the dog, that worried the cat,
That killed the rat, that ate the malt,
That lay in the house that Jack built.

TAFFY was a Welchmen, Taffy was a thief,
    Taffy came to my house and stole a piece
    of beef;
I went to Taffy's house, Taffy wasn't home,
Taffy came to my house and stole a marrow-
    bone;
I went to Taffy's house, Taffy was in bed,
I took the marrow-bone, and beat about his
    head.

BUTTERFLY, butterfly, whence do you
    come?
I know not, I ask not, I never had home.
Butterfly, butterfly, where do you go?
Where the sun shines, and where the buds grow.

HIRAM Gordon, where's your pa?
    He's gone with Uncle Peter,
To put a board across the fence,
    So that we boys can teeter.

JOHN fought for his beloved land,
    And when the war was over,
He kept a little cooky stand,
    And lived and died in clover.

I'VE got a rocket in my pocket,
    I cannot stop to play,
Away she goes, I've burnt my toes,
    'Tis Independence day.

PHOEBE rode a nanny goat,
    Susy broke her leg,
Father took his wedding coat
    And hung it on a peg.

FATHER Short came down the lane,
  Oh, I'm obliged to hammer and smite
  From four in the morning till eight at night,
For a bad master, and a worse dame.

  1. I went up one pair of stairs,
  2. Just like me.
  1. I went up two pair of stairs,
  2. Just like me.
  1. I went into a room,
  2. Just like me.
  1. I looked out of a window,
  2. Just like me.
  1. And then I saw a monkey,
  2. Just like me.

ALL of a row,
  Bend the bow,
Shot at a pigeon,
And killed a crow.

THE cock doth crow,
  To let you know,
If you be well,
'Tis time to rise.

FOR want of a nail, the shoe was lost,
  For want of the shoe, the horse was lost,
For want of the horse, the rider was lost,
For want of the rider, the battle was lost,
For want of the battle, the kingdom was lost,
And all from the want of a horseshoe nail!

BLOW, wind, blow! and go, mill, go!
  That the miller may grind his corn;
That the baker may take it,
And into rolls make it,
  And send us some hot in the morn.

THE Queen of Hearts
    She made some tarts,
  All on a summer's day.
The Knave of Hearts,
He stole the tarts,
  And took them clean away.

The King of Hearts,
Called for the tarts,
  And beat the Knave full sore.
The Knave of Hearts
Brought back the tarts,
  And vow'd he'd steal no more.

ROCK-A-BY, baby, thy cradle is green;
    Father's a nobleman, mother's a queen;
And Betty's a lady, and wears a gold ring;
And Johnny's a drummer, and drums for the
    king.

THERE was a girl in our towne,
    Silk an' satin was her gowne,
Silk an' satin, gold an' velvet,
Guess her name—three times I've tell'd.
                                    [Ann.]

SEE a pin and pick it up,
    All the day you'll have good luck.
See a pin and let it lay,
Bad luck you'll have all the day.

RAIN, Rain, go away;
    Come again another day;
Little Johnny wants to play.

A CAT came fiddling out of a barn,
    With a pair of bag-pipes under her arm:
She could sing nothing but fiddle cum fee,
The mouse has married the humble-bee;
Pipe, cat—dance, mouse,
We'll have a wedding at our good house.

SLEEP, baby, sleep,
    Our cottage vale is deep:
The little lamb is on the green,
With woolly fleece so soft and clean—
    Sleep, baby, sleep.

Sleep, baby, sleep,
Down where the woodbines creep;
Be always like the lamb so mild,
A kind, and sweet, and gentle child.
    Sleep, baby, sleep.

POOR old Robinson Crusoe!
    Poor old Robinson Crusoe!
They made him a coat
Of an old Nanny Goat;
I wonder how they could do so!
    With a ring a ting, tang,
    And a ring a ting, tang,
Poor old Robinson Crusoe!

LITTLE Cock Robin peeped out of his cabin
  To see the cold winter come in.
Tit for tat, what matter for that?
He'll hide his head under his wing!

BLESS you, bless you, bonny bee:
  Say, when will your wedding be?
If it be to-morrow day,
Take your wings and fly away.

BUZ, quoth the blue fly,
  Hum, quoth the bee,
Buz and hum they cry,
  And so do we:
In his ear, in his nose,
  Thus, do you see?
He ate the dormouse,
  Else it was me.

LEND me thy mare to ride a mile?
  " She is lamed, leaping over a stile."
"Alack! and I must keep the fair!
I'll give thee money for thy mare."
"Oh, oh, say you so?
Money will make the mare to go!"

HERE we come gathering nuts and may,
  Nuts and may, nuts and may,
Here we come gathering nuts and may,
On a cold and frosty morning.

PITTY Patty Polt
  Shoe the wild colt;
Here a nail,
And there a nail,
Pitty Patty Polt.

SOLOMON Grundy,
  Born on a Monday,
Christened on Tuesday
Married on Wednesday,
Took ill on Thursday,
Worse on Friday,
Died on Saturday,
Buried on Sunday:
This is the end of
Solomon Grundy.

YEOW mussent sing a' Sunday,
  Becaze it is a sin;
But yeow may sing a' Monday,
  Till Sunday cums agin.

A FROG he would a-wooing go,
    Heigho, says Rowley;
Whether his mother would let him or no:
 With a rowley, powley, gammon, and spinach.
Heigho, says Anthony Rowley.

So off he set with his opera hat,
    Heigho, says Rowley;
And on the road he met a rat,
  With a rowley, powley, &c.

"Pray, Mr. Rat, will you go with me,
    Heigho, says Rowley,
Kind Mrs. Mousey for to see?"
  With a rowley, powley, &c.

When they came to the door at Mousey's hall,
    Heigho, says Rowley,
They gave a loud tap, and they gave a loud call,
  With a rowley, powley, &c.

"Pray, Mrs. Mouse, are you within?"
    Heigho, says Rowley;
"Yes, kind sirs, and sitting to spin."
  With a rowley, powley, &c.

"Pray, Mrs. Mouse, now give us some beer,
    Heigho, says Rowley,
That Froggy and I am fond of good cheer."
  With a rowley, powley, &c.

"Pray, Mr. Frog, will you give us a song?
    Heigho, says Rowley,
But let it be something that's not very long."
  With a rowley, powley, &c.

"Indeed, Mrs. Mouse," replied the Frog,
    Heigho, says Rowley,
"A cold has made me as horse as a hog."
  With a rowley, powley, &c.

"Since you have caught cold, Mr. Frog,"
 Mousey said, [Heigho, says Rowley;
"I'll sing you a song that I have just made.
  With a rowley, powley, &c.

But while they were all a-merrymaking,
     Heigho, says Rowley;
A Cat and her kittens came tumbling in.
   With a rowley, powley, &c.

The Cat she seized the Rat by the crown,
     Heigho, says Rowley,
The kittens they pulled the little Mouse down.
   With a rowley, powley, &c.

This put Mr. Frog in a terrible fright,
     Heigho, says Rowley,
He took up his hat and he wished them good-
 night.]   With a rowley, powley, &c.

As Froggy was crossing it over a brook,
     Heigho, says Rowley,
A lilywhite Duck came and gobbled him up.
   With a rowley, powley, &c.

So here is an end of one, two, three—
     Heigho, says Rowley,
The Rat, the Mouse, and little Froggy.
   With a rowley, powley, &c.

LADIES and gentlemen come to supper,
 Hot boiled beans and very good butter.

[To be sung in a high wind.]

ARTHUR O'Bower has broken his band,
 And he comes roaring up the land,
King of Scots with all his power
Never can turn Sir Arthur O'Bower.

LITTLE Blue Betty lived in a lane,
 She sold good ale to gentlemen:
Gentlemen came every day,
And little Betty Blue hopped away.
She hopped upstairs to make her bed,
And she tumbled down and broke her
 head.

THE North Wind doth blow,
 And we shall have snow,
And what will poor Robin do then?

He will hop to a barn,
And to keep himself warm,
Will hide his head under his wing,
     Poor thing!

THE rose is red, the grass is green;
 And in this book my name is seen.

THERE was an old woman, as I've heard tell,
    She went to market her eggs for to sell;
She went to market all on a market day,
And she fell asleep on the king's highway.

By came a peddler, whose name was Stout,
He cut her petticoats all round about;
He cut her petticoats up to the knees,
Which made the old woman to shiver and freeze.

When the little old women first did wake,
She began to shiver, and she began to shake;
She began to wonder, and she began to cry,
"Lauk a mercy on me, this can't be I!

"But if it be I, as I hope it be,
I've a little dog at home, and he'll know me:
If it be I, he'll wag his little tail,
And if it be not I, he'll loudly bark and wail."

Home went the little woman all in the dark,
Up got the little dog, and he began to bark;
He began to bark, so she began to cry,
"Lauk a mercy on me, this is none of I."

[In the following, the various parts of the countenance are touched
    as the lines are repeated; and at the close the chin is struck play-
    fully, that the tongue may be gently bitten.]

EYE winker,
    Tom Tinker,
    Nose dropper.
Mouth eater,
Chinchopper,
    Chinchopper.

BLACK we are, but much admired;
    Men seek for us till they are tired.
We tire the horse, but comfort man:
Tell me this riddle if you can.
                                    [Coals.]

I LOVE sixpence, pretty little sixpence,
  I love sixpence better than my life;
I spent a penny of it, I spent another,
  And I took fourpence home to my wife.

Oh, my little fourpence, pretty little fourpence,
  I love fourpence better than my life;
I spent a penny of it, I spent another,
And I took twopence home to my wife.

Oh, my little twopence, pretty little twopence,
  I love twopence better than my life;
I spent a penny of it, I spent another,
  And I took nothing home to my wife.

Oh, my little nothing, my pretty little nothing,
  What will nothing buy for my wife?
I have nothing, I spent nothing,
  I love nothing better than my wife.

JEANNIE, come tie my,
  Jeannie, come tie my,
Jeannie, come tie my bonnie cravat;
  I've tied it behind,
  I've tied it before,
And I've tied it so often I'll tie it no more.

THERE was an old soldier of Bister
  Went walking one day with his sister,
When a cow at one poke
Tossed her into an oak,
Before the old gentleman missed her.

CUCKOO, cherry-tree,
  Catch a bird, and give it to me;
Let the tree be high or low,
Let it hail, rain, or snow.

A LITTLE boy went into a barn,
  And lay down on some hay;
An owl came out and flew about,
  And the little boy ran away.

HURLY, burly, trumpet trase,
  The cow was in the market-place.
Some go far, and some go near,
But where shall this poor henchman steer?

I DOUBT, I doubt my fire's all out,
  My little dame is not at home?
I'll saddle my cock, and bridle my hen,
And fetch my little dame home again!

THE rose is red, the violet is blue,
  The gillyflower is sweet and so are you:
These are the words you bade me say
For a pair of new gloves on Easter-day.

JACK be nimble, Jack be quick,
  And Jack jump over the candlestick.

COME when you're called,
  Do what you're bid;
Shut the door after you,
  Never be chid.

SEE-saw Jack in the hedge,
  Which is the way to London Bridge?

WHEN I was a little girl, I washed my
  mammy's dishes;
Now I am a great girl, I roll in golden riches.

"YAUP, yaup, yaup!"
  Said the croaking voice of a Frog:
"A rainy day
In the month of May,
And plenty of room in the bog."

"Yaup, yaup, yaup!"
Said the Frog, as it hopped away;
  "The insects feed
  On the floating weed,
And I'm hungry for dinner to-day."

"Yaup, yaup, yaup!"
Said the Frog, as it splashed about:
  "Good neighbors all,
  When you hear me call,
It is odd that you do not come out."

"Yaup, yaup, yaup!"
Said the Frog; "it is charming weather
  We'll come and sup,
  When the moon is up,
And we'll all of us croak together."

I HAD a little nut-tree, nothing would it bear
But a silver nutmeg and a golden pear;
The king of Spain's daughter came to visit me,
And all was because of my little nut-tree.
I skipped over water, I danced over sea,
And all the birds in the air couldn't catch me.

I WENT to the wood and got it;
I sat me down and looked at it;
The more I looked at it the less I liked it,
And I brought it home because I couldn't
help it.   [A thorn.]

IF I had a donkey that wouldn't go,
Wouldn't I wallop him? Oh, no, no!

IF ifs and ands
Were pots and pans,
There would be no need for tinkers!

PICKELEEM, pickleem, pummis-stone!
What is the news, my beautiful one?
My pet doll-baby, Frances Maria,
Suddenly fainted, and fell in the fire;
The clock on the mantle gave the alarm,
But all we could save was one china arm.

COCKS crow in the morn,
To tell us to rise.
And he who lies late
Will never be wise:

For early to bed,
And early to rise,
Is the way to be healthy
And wealthy and wise.

I HAD two pigeons bright and gay;
They flew from me the other day;
What was the reason they did go?
I cannot tell for I do not know.

I HAD four brothers over the sea.
  Perrie, Merrie, Dixie, Dominie.
And they each sent a present unto me,
  Petrum, Partrum, Paradise, Temporie,
  Perrie, Merrie, Dixie, Dominie.

The first sent a chicken, without any bones;
The second sent a cherry, without any stones,
  Petrum, Partrum, Paradise, Temporie,
  Perrie, Merrie, Dixie, Dominie.

The third sent a book, which no man could read;
The fourth sent a blanket, without any thread.
  Petrum, Partrum, Paradise, Temporie,
  Perrie, Merrie, Dixie, Dominie.

How could there be a chicken without any
  bones?
How could there be a cherry without any
  stones?
  Petrum, Partrum, Paradise, Temporie,
  Perrie, Merrie, Dixie, Dominie.

How could there be a book which no man
  could read?
How could there be a blanket, without a
  thread?
  Petrum, Partrum, Paradise, Temporie,
  Perrie, Merrie, Dixie, Dominie.

When the chicken's in the egg-shell, there are
  no bones,
When the cherry's in the blossom, there are no
  stones.
  Petrum, Partrum, Paradise, Temporie,
  Perrie, Merrie, Dixie, Dominie.

When the book's in ye press no man it can
  read;
When the wool is on the sheep's back, there is
  no thread.
  Petrum, Partrum, Paradise, Temporie,
  Perrie, Merrie, Dixie, Dominie.

I LOVE my love with an A, because he's
  Agreeable.
I hate him because he's Avaricious.
He took me to the Sign of the Acorn,
And treated me with Apples.
His name's Andrew,
And he lives at Arlington.
[This can be continued through the alphabet.]

AS soft as silk, as white as milk,
  As bitter as gall, a thick wall,
And a green coat covers me all.
[A walnut.]

MULTIPLICATION is vexation,
    Division is as bad;
The Rule of Three doth puzzle me,
And Fractions drive me mad.

THEY that wash on Monday
    Have all the week to dry;
They that wash on Tuesday
    Are not so much awry;
They that wash on Wednesday
    Are not so much to blame;
They that wash on Thursday
    Wash for shame;
They that wash on Friday
    Wash in need;
And they that wash on Saturday
    Oh! they're sluts indeed.

CHARLEY, Charley, stole the barley
    Out of the baker's shop;
The baker came out, and gave him a clout,
    And made poor Charley hop.

ONCE I saw a little bird
    Come hop, hop, hop;
So I cried, "Little bird,
    Will you stop, stop, stop?"
And was going to the window,
    To say how do you do;
But he shook his little tail,
    And far away he flew!

HEY diddle, dinketty, pompetty, pet,
    The merchants of London they wear
        scarlet;
Silk in the collar, and gold in the hem,
So merrily march the merchantmen.

WHERE was a jewel and pretty,
    Where was a sugar and spicey?
Hush a bye babe in the cradle,
    And we'll go abroad in a tricey.

Did his papa torment it?
    And vex his own baby will he?
Give me a hand and I'll beat him,
    With your red coral and whistle.

Here we go up, up, up,
    And here we go down, down, downy,
And here we go backward and foreward,
    And here we go round, round, roundy.

FLOUR of England, fruit of Spain,
    Met together in a shower of rain;
Put in a bag tied round with a string,
If you'll tell me this riddle, I'll give you a ring.
                [A plum pudding.]

LITTLE Bob Snooks was fond of his books,
    And loved by his usher and master;
But naughty Jack Spry, he got a black eye,
    And carries his nose in a plaster.

A MAN of words and not of deeds,
    Is like a garden full of weeds;
For when the the weeds begin to grow,
Then doth the garden overflow.

YOU shall have an apple,
    You shall have a plum,
You shall have a rattle-basket,
    When papa comes home.

HIGGLEDY, piggledy
    Here we lie,
Pick'd and pluck'd,
    And put in a pie.
My first is snapping, snarling, growling,
My second's industrious, romping and prowling,
Higgledy piggledy
    Here we lie,
Pick'd and pluck'd
    And put in a pie.
                [Currant.]

I SAW three ships come sailing by,
  Sailing by, sailing by,
I saw three ships come sailing by,
  On New-Year's Day in the morning.

And what do you think was in them then,
  Was in them then, was in them then,
And what do you think was in them then,
  On New-Year's Day in the morning.

Three pretty girls were in them then,
  Were in them then, were in them then,
Three pretty girls were in them then,
  On New-Year's Day in the morning.

And one could whistle, and one could sing,
  And one could play on the violin,
Such joy there was at my wedding,
  On New-Year's Day in the morning.

THE land was white,
  The sea was black;
It'll take a good scholar
To riddle me that.

Paper and writing.

I WILL sing you a song,
  Though 'tis not very long,
Of the woodcock and the sparrow,
Of the little dog that burned his tail,
And he shall be whipped to-morrow.

LITTLE Jack-a-Dandy
  Wanted sugar candy,
And fairly for it cried;
  But little Bill Cook,
  Who always read his book,
Shall have a horse to ride.

LITTLE-BO-PEEP has lost her sheep,
  And can't tell where to find them;
Let them alone, and they'll come home,
  And bring their tails behind them.

Little Bo-Peep fell fast asleep,
  And dreamt she heard them bleating:
But when she awoke she found it a joke,
  For still they all were fleeting.

Then up she took her little crook,
  Determined for to find them;   [bleed,
She found 'em indeed, but it made her heart
  For they'd left their tails behind 'em.

It happened one day, as Bo-Peep did stray
  Unto a meadow hard by,
There she espied their tails, side by side,
  All hung on a tree to dry.

Then she heaved a sigh, and whiped her eye,
  And ran o'er hill and dale-o,   [should,
And tried what she could, as a sheperdess
  To tack to each sheep its tail-o.

CURRAHOO, curr dhoo,
  Love me, and I'll love you!
    [Imitate a Pigeon.]

JOHNNY shall have a new bonnet,
  And Johnny shall go to the fair,
And Johnny shall have a blue ribbon
  To tie up his bonny brown hair.

And why may not I love Johnny?
  And why may not Johnny love me?
And why may not I love Johnny,
  As well as another body?

And here's a leg of a stocking,
  And here is a leg for a shoe,
And he has a kiss for his daddy,
  And two for his mammy, I trow.

And why may not I love Johnny?
  And why may not Johnny love me?
And why may not I love Johnny,
  As well as another body.

SNEEZE on Monday, sneeze for danger;
  Sneeze on Tuesday, kiss a stranger;
Sneeze on Wednesday, receive a letter;
Sneeze on Thursday, something better;
Sneeze on Friday, expect sorrow;
Sneeze on Saturday, joy to-morrow.

A FOX went out in a hungry plight,
  And he begg'd of the moon to give him
    light,
For he'd many miles to trot that night
  Before he could reach his den, O!

At first he came to a farmer's yard,
Where the ducks and the Geese declared it
    hard
That their nerves should be shaken and their
      rest be marr'd,
  By the visit of Mister Fox, O!

He took the gray goose by the sleeve,
Says he, "Madam Goose, and by your leave,
I'll take you away without reprieve,
  And carry you home to my den, O!"

He seized the black duck by the neck,
And swung her all across his back,
The black duck cried out "Quack! quack!
    quack!"
  With her legs hanging dangling down, O!

Then old Mrs. Slipper-Slopper jump'd out of
    bed,
And out of the window she popp'd her head,—
"John, John, John, the gray goose is gone,
  And the fox is off to his den, O!"

Then John he went up to the hill,
And he blew a blast both loud and shrill,
Says the fox, "This is very pretty music—still
  I'd rather be at my den, O!"

At last the fox got home to his den;
To his dear little foxes, eight, nine, ten,
Says he, "You're in luck, here's a good fat
    duck,
  With her legs hanging dangling down, O!"

He then sat down with his hungry wife,
They did very well without fork or knife,
They never ate a better goose in all their life,
  And the little ones pick'd the bones. O?

UP street, and down street,
Each window's made of glass;
If you go to Tommy Tickler's house,
You'll find a pretty lass.

TO market, to market, to buy a plum cake,
Home again, home again, market is late;
To market, to market, to buy a plum bun,
Home again, home again, market is done.

MISS Jane had a bag, and a mouse was in it,
She opened the bag, he was out in a minute,
The cat saw him jump, and run under the table,
And the dog said, catch him, puss, soon as you're able.

MARGERY Mutton-pie and Johnny Bo-peep,
They met together in Gracechurch-Street;
In and out, in and out, over the way,
Oh! says Johnny, 'tis chop-nose day.

HICK-A-MORE, Hack-a-more,
On the king's kitchen-door;
All the king's horses,
And all the king's men,
Couldn't drive Hick-a-more Hack-a-more,
Off the king's kitchen-door!

[Sunshine.]

"JOHN, come sell thy fiddle,
And buy thy wife a gown."
"No, I'll not sell my fiddle,
For ne'er a wife in town."

BONNY lass, pretty lass, wilt thou be mine?
Thou shalt not wash dishes,
Nor yet serve the swine;
Thou shalt sit on a cushion, and sew a fine seam,
And thou shalt eat strawberries, sugar and cream!

THE fox and his wife they had a great strife,
They never ate mustard in all their whole
life;
They ate their meat without fork or knife,
And loved to be picking a bone, e-ho!

The fox jumped up on a moonlight night;
The stars they were shining, and all things
bright;
Oh, ho! said the fox, it's a very fine night
For me to go through the town, e-ho!

The fox when he came to yonder stile,
He lifted his lugs and he listened awhile!
Oh, ho! said the fox its but a short mile
From this unto yonder wee town, e-ho!

The fox when he came to the farmer's gate,
Who should he see but the farmer's drake;
I love you well for your master's sake
And long to be picking your bone, e-ho!

The grey goose she ran round the hay-stack,
Oh, ho! said the fox, you are very fat;
You'll grease my beard and ride on my back
From this into yonder wee town, e-ho!

Old Grammer Hipple-hopple hopped out of
bed,
She opened the casement, and popped out her
head;
Oh! husband, oh! husband, the grey goose is
dead,
And the fox is gone through the town, Oh!

Then the old man got up in his red cap,
And swore he would catch the fox in a
trap;
But the fox was too cunning, and gave him
the slip,
And ran through the town, the town, Oh!

When he got to the top of the hill,
He blew his trumpet both loud and shrill,
For joy that he was safe
Through the town, Oh!

When the fox came back to his den,
He had young ones both nine and ten,
"You're welcome home, daddy; you may go
again,
If you bring us such nice meat
From the town, Oh!"

MARY had a little lamb
　　With fleece as white as snow,
And everywhere that Mary went
　　The lamb was sure to go.

It followed her to school one day,
　　That was against the rule;
It made the children laugh and play,
　　To see a lamb at school.

And so the teacher turned it out,
　　But still it lingered near,
And waited patiently about
　　Till Mary did appear.

"Why does the lamb love Mary so?"
　　The eager children cry.
"Why, Mary loves the lamb, you know!"
　　The teacher did reply.

DRAW a pail of water
　　For my lady's daughter;
My father's a king, and my mother's a queen,
My two little sisters are dressed in green,
Slumping grass and parsley,
Marigold leaves and daisies.
One rush! Two rush!
Pray thee, fine lady, come under my rush

THERE was a little boy and a little girl
　　Lived in our alley;
Says the little boy to the little girl,
　　"Shall I, oh, shall I?"
Says the little girl to the little boy,
　　"What shall we do?"
Says the little boy to the little girl,
　　"I will kiss you!"

A CERTAIN young farmer of Ayr,
　　Started with some sheep for the fair.
He reached the new bridge of Dover,
And, leaving his sheep, went over.
At the end of the bridge is an inn,
Where often before he had been;
Of the inns in the town 'twas the best,
And the farmer said, "Here I will rest."
The number of sheep was so great,
So narrow, too, was the sheep-gate,
That to get them all over, and where
Was resting the farmer of Ayr,
Will take us nine days, maybe ten;
The story must stop until then.

A ENA, deena, dina, duss,
　　Kattle, weela, wila, wuss,
Spit, spot, must be done,
Twiddlum, twaddlum, twenty-one.
O-u-t spells out!

A LL around the green gravel,
　　The grass grows so green,
And all the pretty maids are fit to be seen;
Wash them in milk,
Dress them in silk,
And the first to go down shall be married.

T HE hart he loves the high wood,
　　The hare she loves the hill;
The Knight he loves his bright sword,
The Lady—loves her will.

P LAY, play every day,
　　Harry throws his time away.
He must work and he must read,
And then he'll be a man indeed.

A S the days grow longer
　　The storms grow stronger.

I 'LL tell you a story,
　　About John-a-Nory:
And now my story's begun.
I'll tell you another,
About Jack and his brother,
And now my story's done.

1 He loves me,
2 He don't!
3 He'll have me,
4 He won't!
5 He would if he could,
6 But he can't,
7 So he don't!

THE first day of Christmas,
    My true love sent to me
A partridge in a pear-tree.

The second day of Christmas,
My true love sent to me
Two turtle-doves, and
A partridge in a pear-tree.

The third day of Christmas,
My true love sent to me
Three French hens,
Two turtle-doves, and
A partridge in a pear-tree.

The fourth day of Christmas,
My true love sent to me
Four colly birds,
Three French hens,
Two turtle-doves, and
A partridge in a pear-tree.

The fifth day of Christmas,
My true love sent to me
Five gold rings,
Four colly birds,
Three French hens,
Two turtle-doves, and
A partridge in a pear-tree.

The sixth day of Christmas,
My true love sent to me
Six geese a-laying,
Five gold rings,
Four colly birds,
Three French hens,
Two turtle-doves, and
A partridge in a pear-tree.

The seventh day of Christmas,
My true love sent to me
Seven swans a-swimming,
Six geese a-laying,
Five gold rings,
Four colly birds,
Three French hens,
Two turtle-doves, and
A partridge in a pear-tree.

The eighth day of Christmas,
My true love sent to me
Eight maids a-milking,
Seven swans a-swimming,
Six geese a-laying,
Five gold rings,
Four colly birds,
Three French hens,

Two turtle-doves, and
A partridge in a pear-tree.

The ninth day of Christmas,
My true love sent to me
Nine drummers drumming,
Eight maids a-milking,
Seven swans a-swimming,
Six geese a-laying,
Five gold rings,
Four colly birds,
Three French hens,
Two turtle-doves, and
A partridge in a pear-tree.

The tenth day of Christmas,
My true love sent to me
Ten pipers piping,
Nine drummers drumming,
Eight maids a-milking,
Seven swans a-swimming,
Six geese a-laying,
Five gold rings,
Four colly birds,
Three French hens,
Two turtle-doves, and
A partridge in a pear-tree.

The eleventh day of Christmas,
My true love sent to me
Eleven ladies dancing,
Ten pipers piping,
Nine drummers drumming,
Eight maids a-milking,
Seven swans a-swimming,
Six geese a-laying,
Five gold rings,
Four colly birds,
Three French hens,
Two turtle-doves, and
A partridge in a pear-tree.

The twelfth day of Christmas,
My true love sent to me
Twelve lords a-leaping,
Eleven ladies dancing,
Ten pipers piping,
Nine drummers drumming,
Eight maids a-milking,
Seven swans a-swimming,
Six geese a-laying,
Five gold rings,
Four colly birds,
Three French hens,
Two turtle-doves, and
A partridge in a pear-tree.

PEASE porridge hot,
  Pease porridge cold,
Pease porridge in the pot nine days old.
Some like it hot,
Some like it cold,
Some like it in the pot nine days old.
Spell me *that* with a P
And a clever scholar you will be.

THE two gray kits,
  And the gray kits' mother
All went over
The bridge together.
The bridge broke down,
They all fell in;
May the rats go with you,
Says Tom Robin.

UP hill and down dale;
  Butter is made in every vale;
And if that Nancy Cook
Is a good girl,
She shall have a spouse,
And make butter anon,
Before her old grandmother
Grows a young man.

HERE stands a post,—
  Who put it there?
A better man than you:
  Touch it if you dare?

A HILL full—a hole full
  Yet you cannot catch a bowl full.
[Mist.]

CRY, baby, cry,
  Put your finger in your eye,
And tell your mother it wasn't I.

GREAT A, little A,
  This is pancake day;
Toss the ball high,
Throw the ball low,
Those that come after
May sing Heigh-ho!

Pease porridge hot, pease porridge cold, Pease porridge in the pot, nine days old.

(Page 118)

HECTOR Protector was dressed all in green;
  Hector Protector was sent to the Queen.
The Queen did not like him,
No more did the King:
So Hector Protector was sent back again.

HERE'S Sulky Sue,
  What shall we do?
Turn her face to the wall
Till she comes to.

LOVE your own, kiss your own,
  Love your own mother, hinny,
For if she was dead and gone,
  You'd ne'er get such another hinny.

JANUARY brings the snow,
  Makes our feet and fingers glow.

February brings the rain,
Thaws the frozen lake again.

March brings breezes loud and shrill,
Stirs the dancing daffodil.

April brings the primrose sweet,
Scatters daisies at our feet.

May brings flocks of pretty lambs,
Skipping by their fleecy dams.

June brings tulips, lilies, roses,
Fills the chidren's hands with posies.

Hot July brings cooling showers,
Apricots and gillyflowers.

August brings the sheaves of corn,
Then the harvest home is borne.

Warm September brings the fruit,
Sportsmen then begin to shoot.

Fresh October brings the pheasant.
Then to gather nuts is pleasant.

Dull November brings the blast,
Then the leaves are whirling fast.

Chill December brings the sleet,
Blazing fire and Christmas treat.

AN old woman was sweeping her house, and she found a little crooked sixpence. "What," said she, "shall I do with this little sixpence? I will go to market, and buy a little pig." As she was coming home, she came to a stile: the piggy would not go over the stile.

She went a little farther, and she met a dog. So she said to the dog—

"Dog, dog, bite pig;
Piggy won't get over the stile;
And I shan't get home to-night."

But the dog would not.
She went a little farther, and she met a stick. So she said—

"Stick, stick, beat dog:
Dog won't bite pig;
Piggy won't get over the stile;
And I shan't get home to-night."

But the stick would not.
She went a little farther, and she met a fire. So she said—

"Fire, fire, burn stick;
Stick won't beat dog;
Dog won't bite pig;
Piggy won't get over the stile;
And I shan't get home to-night."

But the fire would not.
She went a little farther, and she met some water. So she said-

"Water, water, quench fire;
Fire won't burn stick;
Stick won't beat dog;
Dog won't bite pig;
Piggy won't get over the stile;
And I shan't get home to-night."

But the water would not.
She went a little farther, and she met an ox. So she said—

"Ox, ox, drink water;
Water won't quench fire;
Fire won't burn stick;
Stick won't beat dog;

Dog won't bite pig;
Piggy won't get over the stile;
And I shan't get home to-night."

But the ox would not.
She went a little farther, and she met a butcher. So she said—

"Butcher, butcher, kill ox.
Ox won't drink water;
Water won't quench fire;
Fire won't burn stick;
Stick won't beat dog;
Dog won't bite pig;
Piggy won't get over the stile;
And I shan't get home to-night."

But the butcher would not.
She went a little farther, and she met a rope. So she said—

"Rope, rope, hang butcher;
Butcher won't kill ox;
Ox won't drink water;
Water won't quench fire;
Fire won't burn stick;
Stick won't beat dog;
Dog won't bite pig;
Piggy won't get over the stile;
And I shan't get home to-night."

But the rope would not.
She went a little farther, and she met a rat. So she said—

"Rat, rat, gnaw rope;
Rope won't hang butcher;
Butcher won't kill ox;
Ox won't drink water;
Water won't quench fire;
Fire won't burn stick;
Stick won't beat dog;
Dog won't bite pig;
Piggy won't get over the stile;
And I shant get home to-night."

But the rat would not.
She went a little farther, and she met a cat. So she said—

"Cat, cat, kill rat;
Rat won't gnaw rope;
Rope won't hang butcher;
Butcher won't kill ox;
Ox won't drink water;
Water won't quench fire;
Fire won't burn stick;
Stick won't beat dog;
Dog won't bite pig;

Piggy won't get over the stile;
And I shan't get home to-night."

But the cat said to her, "If you will go to yonder cow, and fetch me a saucer of milk, I will kill the rat." So away went the old woman to the cow, and said—

"Cow, cow, give me a saucer of milk;
Cat won't kill rat;
Rat won't gnaw rope;
Rope won't hang butcher;
Butcher won't kill ox;
Ox won't drink water;
Water won't quench fire;
Fire won't burn stick;
Stick won't beat dog;
Dog won't bite pig;
Piggy won't get over the stile;
And I shan't get home to-night;

But the cow said to her, "If you will go to yonder haymakers, and fetch me a wisp of hay, I'll give you the milk." So away the old woman went to the haymakers, and said—

"Haymakers, give me a wisp of hay;
Cow won't give me milk;

Cat won't kill rat;
Rat won't gnaw rope;
Rope won't hang butcher;
Butcher won't kill ox;
Ox won't drink water;
Water won't quench fire;
Fire won't burn stick;
Stick won't beat dog;
Dog won't bite pig;
Piggy won't get over the stile;
And I shan't get home to-night."

But the haymakers said to her,—"If you will go to yonder stream, and fetch us a bucket of water, we will give you the hay." So away the old woman went; but when she got to the stream, she found the bucket was full of holes. So she covered the bottom with pebbles, and then filled the bucket with water, and away she went back with it to the haymakers; and they gave her a wisp of hay.

As soon as the cow had eaten the hay, she gave the old woman the milk; and away she went with it in the saucer to the cat. As soon as the cat had lapped up the milk—

The cat began to kill the rat;
The rat began to gnaw the rope;

The rope began to hang the butcher;
The butcher began to kill the ox:
The ox began to drink the water;
The water began to quench the fire;
The fire began to burn the stick;
The stick began to beat the dog;
The dog began to bite the pig;
The little pig in a fright jumped over the stile;
And so the old woman got home that night.

AS I was going to St. Ives,
I met a man with seven wives,
Every wife had seven sacks,
Every sack had seven cats,
Every cat had seven kits:
Kits, cats, sacks, and wives,
How many were there going to St. Ives?

[One.]

THERE was an old woman
Called Nothing-at-all,
Who rejoiced in a dwelling
Exceedingly small:
A man stretched his mouth
To its utmost extent,
And down at one gulp
House and old woman went.

TOM, Tom, the piper's son,
He learnt to play when he was young.
He with his pipe made such a noise,
That he pleased all the girls and boys.

JOCKEY was a piper's son,
And he fell in love when he was young,
And the only tune he could play
Was, "Over the hills and far away;"
Over the hills and a great way off,
And the wind will blow my top-knot off.

I HAD a little cow;
Hey-diddle, ho-diddle!
I had a little cow, and it had a little calf;
Hey-diddle, ho-diddle; and there's my song
half.

I had a little cow;
Hey-diddle, ho-diddle!
I had a little cow, and I drove it to the stall;
Hey-diddle, ho-diddle; and there's my song all.

SING, sing!—What shall I sing?
The cat's run away with the pudding-
bag string!

A CURIOUS discourse about an Apple-pie, that passed between the Twenty-five Letters at Dinner-time.
Says A, Give me a good large slice.
Says B, A little Bit, but nice.
Says C, Cut me a piece of Crust.
Says D, It is as Dry as Dust.
Says E, I'll Eat now, fast who will.
Says F, I vow I'll have my Fill
Says G, Give it to me Good and Great.
Says H, A little bit I Hate.
Says I, I love the Juice the best.
And K the very same confessed.
Says, L, There's nothing more I Love.
Says M, It makes your teeth to Move.
N, Noticed what the others said.
O, Others' plates with grief surveyed.
P, Praised the cook up to the life.
Q, Quarrelled 'cause he'd a bad knife.
Says R, It Runs short, I'm afraid.
S, silent sat, and nothing said.
T, Thought that Talking might loose time.
U, Understood it at meals a crime.
W, Wished there had been a quince in.
Says X, Those cooks there's no convincing.
Says Y, I'll eat, let others wish.
Z sat as mute as any fish.
While ampersand, he licked the dish.

HAVE you seen the old woman of Banbury Cross,
Who rode to the fair on the top of her horse?
And since her return she still tells, up and down,
Of the wonderful lady she saw when in town,
She has a small mirror in each of her eyes,
And her nose is a bellows of minnikin size;
There's a neat little drum fix'd in each of her ears,
Which beats a tattoo to what ever she hears.
She has in each jaw a fine ivory mill,
And day after day she keeps grinding it still.
Both an organ and flute in her small throat are placed,
And they are played by a steam engine worked in her breast.
But the wonder of all, in her mouth it is said,
She keeps a loud bell that might waken the dead;
And so frightened the woman, and startled the horse,
That they galloped full speed back to Banbury Cross.

IF you are a gentleman, as I suppose you be,
You'll neither laugh nor smile at the tickling of your knee.

THERE was a man and he was mad,
  And he jump'd into a pea-swad; *
The pea-swad was over-full,
So he jump'd into a roaring bull;
The roaring bull was over-fat,
So he jump'd into a gentleman's hat,
The gentleman's hat was over-fine,
So he jump'd into a bottle of wine;
The bottle of wine was over-dear,
So he jump'd into a bottle of beer;

The bottle of beer was over-thick,
So he jump'd into a club-stick;
The club-stick was over-narrow,
So he jump'd into a wheel-barrow;
The wheel-barrow began to crack,
So he jump'd on to a hay-stack;
The hay-stack began to blaze,
So he did nothing but cough and sneeze!

* The pod or shell of a pea

MATTHEW, Mark, Luke and John,
  Bless the bed that I lie on.
Four corners to my bed,
Four angels over head,
One to sing and one to pray,
And two to bear my soul away.

THERE was a little Guinea-pig
  Who, being little, was not big,
He always walked upon his feet,
And never fasted when he ate.

When from a place he ran away,
He never at that place did stay.
And while he ran, as I am told,
He ne'er stood still for young or old.

He often squeaked and sometimes vi'lent,
And when he squeaked he ne'er was silent;
Though ne'er instructed by a cat,
He knew a mouse was not a rat.

One day, as I am certified,
He took a whim and fairly died;
And, as I'm told by men of sense,
He never has been living since.

THERE was a crooked man,
  And he went a crooked mile,
And he found a crooked sixpence
  Against a crooked stile;
He bought a crooked cat,
  Which caught a crooked mouse,
And they all lived together
  In a little crooked house.

LITTLE maid, little maid,
　　Whither goest thou?
Down in the meadow
To milk my cow.

THREE little kittens they lost their
　　And they began to cry,　　　[mittens,
　　　　"Oh! mammy dear,
　　　　We sadly fear,
　　Our mittens we have lost!"
"What! lost your mittens,
You naughty kittens,
　　　Then you shall have no pie."
　　　　Miew, miew, miew, miew,
　　　　Miew, miew, miew, miew.

The three little kittens they found their
And they began to cry,　　　　[mittens,
　　　　"Oh! mammy dear,
　　　　See here, see here,
　　Our mittens we have found.
"What! found your mittens,
You little kittens,
　　　Then you shall have some pie,"
　　　　Purr, purr, purr, purr,
　　　　Purr, purr, purr, purr.

The three little kittens put on their mittens,
And soon ate up the pie;
　　　　"Oh! mammy dear,
　　　　We greatly fear,
　　Our mittens we have soil'd."
"What! soil'd your mittens,
You naughty kittens!"
　　　　Then they began to sigh,
　　　　Miew, miew, miew, miew,
　　　　Miew, miew, miew, miew.

The three little kittens they washed their
And hung them up to dry;　　　[mittens,
　　　　"Oh! mammy dear,
　　　　Look here, look here,
　　Our mittens we have wash'd."
"What! wash'd your mittens,
You darling kittens!
　　　But I smell a rat close by!
　　　　Hush! hush!" Miew, miew,
　　　　Miew, miew, miew, miew.

A JOLLY fat miller in Poopleton Bun,
　　With elephant legs that weigh half a
　　　　ton,
And face that is round, and red as the sun.

WHEN V and I together meet,
　　They make a number Six complete.
When I with V doth meet once more,
Then 'tis they Two can make but Four.
And when that V from I is gone,
Alas! poor I can make but One.

OLD Mother Hubbard
　　Went to the cupboard
　To get her poor Dog a bone;
But when she came there
The cupboard was bare,
　And so the poor Dog had none.

She went to the baker's
　To buy him some bread,
But when she came back
　She thought he was dead.

She went to the joiner's
　To buy him a coffin,
But when she came back
　The sly dog was laughing.

She took a clean dish,
　To get him some tripe,
But when she came back
　He was smoking his pipe.

She went to the ale-house,
　To get him some beer,
But when she came back
　The dog sat in a chair.

She went to the tavern,
　For white wine and red,
But when she came back
　He stood on his head.

She went to the hatter's
　To buy him a hat,
But when she came back
　He was feeding the cat.

She went to the barber's
　To buy him a wig,
But when she came back
　He was dancing a jig.

She went to the fruiterer's
　To buy him some fruit,
But when she came back
　He was playing a flute.

She went to the tailor's,
　To buy him a coat,
But when she came back
　He was riding a goat.

She went to the cobbler's,
  To buy him some shoes,
But when she came back
  He was reading the news

She went to the sempstress,
  To buy him some linen,
But when she came back
  The dog was spinning.

She went to the hosier's,
  To buy him some hose,
But when she came back
  He was dress'd in his clothes.

The Dame made a curtsey,
  The Dog made a bow;
The Dame said "Your servant,"
  The Dog said "Bow wow!"

This wonderful Dog
  Was Dame Hubbard's delight;
He could sing, he could dance,
  He could read, he could write.

She gave him rich dainties
  Whenever he fed,
And erected a monument
  When he was dead.

IN marble walls as white as milk,
  Lined with a skin as soft as silk;
Within a fountain crystal clear,
A golden apple doth appear.
No doors there are to this stronghold—
Yet thieves break in and steal the gold.
                    [An Egg.]

A RIDDLE, a riddle, as I suppose,
  A hundred eyes, and never a nose.
                    [A cinder-sifter.]

DINGTY Diddledy, my mammy's maid,
　　She stole oranges, I am afraid:
Some in her pocket, some in her sleeve,
She stole oranges, I do believe.

RIDE a cock-horse to Banbury Cross,
　　To see a fine lady upon a white
　　　　horse;
With rings on her fingers and bells on her toes,
She shall have music wherever she goes.

EVERY body in this land
　　Has twenty nails upon each hand
Five and twenty hands and feet—
All this is true without deceit.

[Mind your Punctuation.]

I SAW a peacock with a fiery tail,
　　I saw a blazing comet drop down hail,
I saw a cloud wrapped with ivy round,
I saw an oak creep on the ground,
I saw a snail swallow up a whale,
I saw the sea brimful of ale,
I saw a Venice glass full fifteen feet deep,
I saw a well full of men's tears that weep,
I saw red eyes all of a flaming fire,
I saw a house bigger than the moon and higher,
I saw the sun at twelve o'clock at night,
I saw the man that saw this wondrous sight.

TWELVE pears hanging high,
　　Twelve knights riding by—
Each took a pear,
And yet left eleven there.

PETER White
　　Will ne'er go right.
Would you know the reason why?
　　He follows his nose,
　　Wherever he goes,
And that stands all awry.

WHERE should a baby rest?
Where but on its mother's arm—
Where can a baby lie
Half so safe from every harm?
Lulla, lulla, lullaby,
Softly sleep, my baby;
Lulla, lulla, lullaby,
Soft, soft, my baby.

Nestle there, my lovely one!
Press to mine thy velvet cheek;
Sweetly coo, and smile, and look,
All the love thou canst not speak.
Lulla, lulla, lullaby,
Softly sleep, my baby;
Lulla, lulla, lullaby,
Soft, soft, my baby.

TO market, to market, a gallop, a trot,
To buy some meat to put in the pot;
Five cents a quarter, ten cents a side,
If it hadn't been killed, it must have died.

MARY, Mary, quite contrary,
How does your garden grow?
Silver bells and cockle shells,
And pretty maids all in a row.

WHY is pussy in bed, pray?
She is sick, says the fly,
And I fear she will die;
That's why she's in bed.

Pray, what's her disorder?
She's got a locked jaw,
Says the little jackdaw,
And that's her disorder.

Who makes her gruel?
I, says the horse,
For I am her nurse,
And I make her gruel.

Pray, who is her doctor?
Quack, quack! says the duck,
I that task undertook,
And I am her doctor.

Who thinks she'll recover?
I, says the deer,
For I did last year:
So I think she'll recover.

A, B, C, tumble down D,
The cat's in the cupboard, and can't see
me.

LITTLE Queen Pippin once built a hotel,
  How long and how high, I'm sure I
    can't tell;
The walls were of sugar, as white as the snow,
And jujube windows were placed in a row;
The columns were candy, and all very tall,
And a roof of choice cakes was spread over all.

A FROG among some rushes dwelt,
  A bachelor was he;
No Frog was ever so polite,
  Or such a beau could be.

In passing near a cottage, once,
  He chanced to look above,
And there beheld a pretty Mouse,
  With whom he fell in love.

Her eyes and whiskers he admired,
  Her coat of softest fur,
And wished to make her feel for him
  The love—he felt for her.

So he put on his scarf of red,
  His opera hat he wore;
And, hopping to the house, he gave
  A rat-tat at the door.

Mousey, as bashful as a miss,
  Retired from Froggy's view,
But peeped at him, from out her hole,
  As Froggy nearer drew.

Froggy approached and doffed his hat,
  Then, bending on one knee,
Said—"Fairest Mouse, pray listen to
  My tale of love for thee.

"In me, the wretchedest of Frogs,
  You see a love-sick swain;
Oh say—you'll Mistress Froggy be,
  And make me well again.

"A tiny house I have, hard by,
  'Tis built among the rushes:
You shall have dainties, every day,
  With hips from wild-rose bushes."

Miss Mousey simpered and looked prim,
  Then, modestly, she said,
"I do admire your yellow dress,
  And handsome scarf of red.

"Oh, how can I resist that tongue?
  Those eyes of golden red;
Your offer I accept at once,
  And will no other wed."

No more was said, but arm in arm,
　To church they hopped away,
Got married, and prepared a feast
　To grace their wedding day.

And to that wedding feast there came
　Some Frogs of high degree,
And Mice of birth illustrious,
　And first-rate pedigree.

But what it was they feasted on,
　We will not here record,
But, be assured they had the best
　The season could afford.

The feast concluded, toasts went round,
　In water from the rills;
And then eight merry Frogs and Mice
　Got up to dance quadrilles.

A FARMER went trotting upon his gray
　　mare,
　　　　　Bumpety, bumpety, bump;
With his daughter behind him so rosy and fair,
　　　　　Lumpety, lumpety, lump.
A raven cried croak, and they all tumbled down,
　　　　　Bumpety, bumpety, bump;
The mare broke her knees and the Farmer his
　crown,
　　　　　Lumpety, lumpety, lump.
The mischievous raven flew laughing away,
　　　　　Bumpety, bumpety, bump;
And vowed he would serve them the same next
　day,
　　　　　Lumpety, lumpety, lump.

THREE wise men of Gotham,
　Went to sea in a bowl;
If the bowl had been stronger,
My song had been longer.

OLD woman, old woman, shall we go a-
    shearing?
Speak a little louder, sir, I am very thick
    o' hearing.
Old woman, old woman, shall I kiss you
    dearly?
Thank you, kind sir, I hear very clearly.

LUCY Locket lost her pocket,
    Kitty Fisher found it:
Not a penny in it,
But a ribbon 'round it.

HOP away, skip away, my baby wants to
    My baby wants to play every day. [play;

ARITHMETIC I studied so,
    It taught me how to trade;
I sold a yard of calico,
    And now my fortune's made.

THIRTY white horses
    Upon a red hill,
Now they tramp, now they champ,
    Now they stand still.
        [Teeth and Gums.]

I HAD a little hobby horse,
    And it was dapple gray,
Its head was made of pea-straw,
    Its tail was made of hay.
I sold it to an old woman
    For a copper groat;
And I'll not sing my song again
    Without a new coat.

HE that would thrive
    Must rise at five;
He that hath thriven
May lie till seven;
And he that by the plough would thrive,
Himself must either hold or drive.

AS I was going to sell my eggs,
    I met a man with bandy legs—
Bandy legs and crooked toes,
I tripped up his heels, and he fell on his nose.

HOGS in the garden, catch'em Towser;
    Cows in the corn-field, run boys, run;
Cat's in the cream-pot, run girls, run girls;
    Fire on the mountains, run boys, run.

LITTLE Bob Robin, where do you live?
    Up in a wood, sir, on a hazel twig.

I'M in every one's way,
    But no one I stop;
My four horns every day
    In every way play,
And my head is nailed on at the top!
                                    [Turnstile.]

COME dance a jig
    To my Granny's pig,
With a rawdy, rowdy, dowdy;
    Come dance a jig
    To my Granny's pig,
And pussy-cat shall crowdy.

SING song! merry go round,
    Here we go up to the moon, Oh!
Little Johnnie a penny has found,
    And so we'll sing a tune, Oh!
        What shall I buy?
        Johnnie did cry,
With the penny I've found
So bright and round?
What shall you buy?
A kite that will fly
Up to the moon, all through the sky!
But if, when it gets there,
It should stay in the air,
Or the man in the moon
Should open the door,
And take it in with his long, long paw,—
We should sing to another tune, Oh!

ABOUT the bush, Willie, about the bee-hive,
    About the bush, Willie, I'll meet thee alive.

JOHNNY'S too little to whittle,
  Give him some raspberry jam,
Take off his bib, put him into his crib,
  And feed him on doughnuts and ham.

THERE was an old woman tossed up in a
  basket,
  Ninety times as high as the moon:
And where she was going, I couldn't but ask
    her,
  For in her her hand she carried a broom.

"Old woman, old woman, old woman,"
    quoth I,
  "Wither, O wither, O wither so high?"
"To sweep the cobwebs off the sky!"
  "Shall I go with you?" "Aye, by-and-by."

JOHN O'Gudgeon was a wild man,
  He whipped his children now and then.
When he whipped them he made them dance
Out of England into France.

I HAD a little boy,
  And called him Blue Bell;
Gave him a little work,—
  He did it very well.

I bade him go upstairs
  To bring me a gold pin;
In coal scuttle fell he,
  Up to his little chin.

He went to the garden
  To pick a little sage;
He tumbled on his nose,
  And fell into a rage.

He went to the cellar
  To draw a little beer;
And quickly did return
  To say there was none there.

SEE, see. What shall I see?
  A horse's head where his tail should be.

A was an Archer, and shot at a frog.

B was a Butcher, and had a great dog.

C was a Captain, all covered with lace.

D was a Dunce, with a very sad face.

E was an Esquire, with pride on his brow,

F was a Farmer, and followed the plough.

G was a Gamester, who had but ill-luck,

H was a hunter, and hunted a buck.

I was an Innkeeper, who lov'd to bouse,

J was a Joiner, and built up a house.

K was a King, so mighty and grand,

L was a Lady, who had a white hand.

M was a Miser, who hoarded up his gold,

N was a Nobleman, gallant and bold.

O was an Oysterman, and went about town,

P was a Parson, and wore a black gown.

Q was a Quack, with a wonderful pill,

R was a Robber, who wanted to kill.

S was a Sailor, and spent all he got,

T was a Tinker, and mended a pot.

U was an Usurer, a miserable elf,

V was a Vintner, who drank all himself.

W was a Watchman, and guarded the door,

X was expensive, and so became poor.

Y was a Youth, that did not love school,

Z was a Zan, a poor harmless fool.

LAZY Tom, with jacket blue,
  Stole his father's gouty shoe;
The worst of harm we can wish him,
  Is, his gouty shoe may fit him.

INTERY, mintery, cutery, corn,
  Apple seed, and apple thorn;
Wine, brier, limber lock,
Three geese in a flock,
One flew east, one flew west,
And one flew over the goose's nest.

PEG, Peg, with a wooden leg—
  Her father was a miller;
He tossed the dumpling at her head,
  And said he could not kill her.

HOW many days has my baby to play?
  Saturday, Sunday, Monday,
Tuesday, Wednesday, Thursday, Friday,
Saturday, Sunday, Monday.

CLAP hands, clap hands!
  Till father comes home:
For father's got money,
  But mother's got none.
    Clap hands, &c.

MISS one, two and three could never
  agree,
While they gossiped round a tea-caddy.

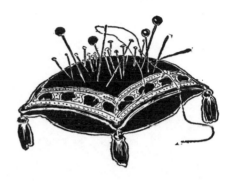

NEEDLES and pins, needles and pins,
  When a man marries, his trouble
    begins.

SHOE the horse, and shoe the mare,
  But let the little colt go bare.

THERE was a fat man of Bombay,
  Who was smoking one sunshiny
    day;
  When a bird, called a snipe,
  Flew away with his pipe,
Which vex'd the fat man of Bombay.

HANDY Spandy, Jack a-dandy,
  Loves plum-cake and sugar candy;
He bought some at a grocer's shop,
And out he came, hop-hop-hop.

DOCTOR Foster went to Gloster,
  In a shower of rain
He stepped in a puddle,
Up to the middle,
  And never went there again.

JACK Sprat
  Had a cat,
It had but one ear;
  It went to buy butter
When butter was dear.

HERE goes my lord
  A trot, a trot, a trot,
Here goes my lady
A canter, a canter, a canter, a canter!
  Here goes my young master
Jockey-hitch, Jockey-hitch, Jockey-hitch,
  Jockey-hitch!
  Here goes my young miss,
An amble, an amble, an amble, an amble!
The footman lags behind to tipple ale and wine,
And goes gallop, a gallop, a gallop, to make up
  his time.

SEE saw, Margery Daw,
  Jenny shall have a new master;
She shall have but a penny a-day,
  Because she can't work any faster.

ROSEMARY green, and lavender blue,
  Thyme and sweet majorum, hyssop and
  rue.

PUSSY Cat Mole,
  Jump'd over a Coal,
And in her best petticoat burnt a great hole.
Poor pussy's weeping, she'll have no more milk
Until her best petticoat's mended with silk.

TRIP and go, heave and ho!
  Up and down, to and fro;
From the town to the grove,
Two and two, let us rove,
A-maying, a-playing;
Love hath no gainsaying!
  So merrily trip and go!
  So merrily trip and go!

TWO little dogs
  Sat by the fire,
Over a fender of coal-dust;
Said one little dog
To the other little dog,
  If you don't talk, why, I must.

RIDDLE me, riddle me, ree,
  A hawk sate upon a tree;
And he says to himself, says he,
Oh dear! What a fine bird I be!

YOUNG Lambs to sell!
  Young Lambs to sell!
If I'd as much money as I can tell,
I never would cry Young Lambs to sell!

THERE was an old woman who rode on a
      broom,
  With a high gee ho, gee humble;
And she took her old cat behind for a groom,
  With a bimble, bamble, bumble—

They travelled along till they came to the sky,
  With a high gee ho, gee humble;
But the journey so long made them very hungry,
  With a bimble, bamble, bumble—

Says her cat, "I can find something here to eat,"
  With a high gee ho, gee humble;
So let's go back again, I entreat,
  With a bimble, bamble, bumble—

The old woman would not go back so soon,
  With a high gee ho, gee humble;
For she wanted to visit the Man in the Moon,
  With a bimble, bamble, bumble—

Says the cat, "I'll go back myself to our house,
  With a high gee ho, gee humble;
For there I can catch a good rat or a mouse,
  With a bimble, bamble, bumble.

IT'S raining, it's pouring,
  The old man is snoring

SOME little mice sat in a barn to spin,
Pussy came by, and she popped her head in;
"Shall I come in and cut your threads off?"
"Oh no, kind sir, you will snap our heads off."

ROBIN Hood, Robin Hood,
Is in the mickle wood!
Little John, Little John,
He to the town is gone.
Robin Hood, Robin Hood,
Is telling his beads,
All in the greenwood,
Among the green weeds.
Little John, Little John,
If he comes no more,
Robin Hood, Robin Hood,
We shall fret full sore!

FOUR and twenty tailors
Went to kill a snail;
The best man amongst them
Durst not touch her tail.
She put out her horns,
Like a little Keyloe cow;
Run, tailors run,
Or she'll catch you all just now.

WHO killed Cock Robin?
I, said the Sparrow,
With my bow and arrow,
I killed Cock Robin

Who saw him die?
I, said the Fly,
With my little eye,
I saw him die.

Who caught his blood?
I, said the Fish,
With my little dish,
I caught his blood.

Who'll make his shroud?
  I, said the Beetle,
  With my thread and needle,
I'll make his shroud.

Who'll dig his grave?
  I, said the Owl,
  With my spade and show'l,
I'll dig his grave.

Who'll be the Parson?
  I, said the Rook,
  With my little book,
I'll be the Parson.

Who'll be the Clerk?
  I, said the Lark,
  If it's not in the dark
  I'll be the Clerk.

Who'll carry him to the grave?
  I, said the Kite,
  If it's not in the night,
I'll carry him to the grave.

Who'll carry the link?
  I, said the Linnet,
  I'll fetch it in a minute,
I'll carry the link.

Who'll be chief mourner?
  I, said the Dove,
  For I mourn for my love,
I'll be chief mourner.

Who'll sing a psalm?
  I, said the Thrush,
  As she sat in a bush,
I'll sing a psalm.

Who'll toll the bell?
  I, said the Bull,
  Because I can pull;
So, Cock Robin, farewell.

All the birds of the air
  Fell a-sighing and sobbin',
When they heard the bell toll
  For Poor Cock Robin.

UPON my word and honor,
  As I went to Bonner
I met a pig,
Without a wig,
Upon my word and honor.

SNAIL, Snail, come out of your hole,
    Or else I'll beat you black as a coal.
Snail, Snail, put out your head,
Or else I'll beat you till you're dead.

AWAKE, arise, pull out your eyes,
    And hear what time of day;
And when you have done,
Pull out your tongue,
    And see what you can say.

[A Chimney.]

BLACK within, and red without;
    Four corners round about.

TO make your candles last forever,
    You wives and maids give ear-o!
To put them out is the only way,
    Says honest John Boldero.

A GOOD child, a good child,
    As I suppose you be;
Never laugh nor smile,
    At the tickling of your knee.

OLD father Grey Beard,
    Without tooth or tongue;
If you'll give me your finger,
I'll give you my thumb.

THE man in the wilderness asked me,
    How many strawberries grew in the sea?
I answered him, as I thought good,
As many as red herrings grew in the wood.

AWAY, birds, away!
    Take a little, and leave a little,
And do not come again;
For if you do,
I will shoot you through,
And then there will be an end of you.

WILLY boy, Willy boy,
   Where are you going?
I will go with you, if I may.
I am going to the meadows,
   To see them mowing,
I am going to see them make hay.

HEIGH ding-a-ding, what shall I sing?
   How many holes in a skimmer?
Four and twenty. I'm half starving!
   Mother, pray give me some dinner.

BAT, bat, come under my hat,
   And I'll give you a slice of bacon;
And when I bake, I'll give you a cake,
   If I am not mistaken.

MY little old man and I fell out,
   I'll tell you what 'twas all about:
I had money and he had none,
   And that's the way the noise begun.

HUMPTY-Dumpty sat on a wall,
   Humpty-Dumpty had a great fall;
All the king's horses, and all the king's men,
Cannot put Humpty-Dumpty together again.

                              [An Egg.]

TOMMY Trot, a man of laws,
   Sold his bed and lay upon straws;
Sold the straw, and slept on grass,
To buy his wife a looking-glass.

LITTLE Tee Wee,
   He went to sea,
In an open boat;
And while afloat
The little boat bended.
My story's ended.

HICKETY, pickety, my black hen,
   She lays good eggs for gentlemen;
Gentlemen come every day,
To see what my black hen doth lay.

GOOD people all, of every sort,
  Give ear unto my song:
And if you find it wondrous short,
  It cannot hold you long.

In Islington there was a man,
  Of whom the world might say,
That still a Godly race he ran,
  Whene'er he went to pray.

A kind and gentle heart he had,
  To comfort friends and foes;
The naked every day he clad,
  When he put on his clothes.

And in that town a dog was found:
  As many dogs there be—
Both mongrel, puppy, whelp, and hound,
  And curs of low degree.

This dog and man at first were friends,
  But, when a pique began,
The dog, to gain some private ends,
  Went mad, and bit the man.

Around from all the neighboring streets
  The wondering neighbors ran;
And swore the dog had lost his wits,
  To bite so good a man.

The wound it seemed both sore and sad
  To every Christian eye;
And while they swore the dog was mad,
  They swore the man would die.

But soon a wonder came to light,
  That showed the rogues they lied—
The man recovered of the bite;
  The dog it was that died.

I HAVE been to market, my lady, my lady.
  Then you've not been to the fair, says
  pussy, says pussy.
I bought me a rabbit, my lady, my lady.
Then you did not buy a hare, says pussy, says
  pussy.

THERE was a maid on Scrabble Hill,
  And if not dead, she lives there still;
She grew so tall, she reached the sky,
And on the moon hung clothes to dry.

BARNEY Bodkin broke his nose;
  Without feet we can't have toes.
Crazy folks are always mad.
Want of money makes us sad.

OLD Boniface, he loved good cheer
  And drank his glass of Burton;
And when the nights grew sultry hot,
He slept without a shirt on.

MY father he died, but I can't tell you how;
  He left me six horses to drive in my
    plough;
  With my wing, wang, waddle O,
  Jack sing saddle O,
  Blowsey boys bubble O,
  Under the broom.

I sold my six horses, and bought me a cow,
I'd fain have made a fortune, but did not know
    how;
  With my wing, wang, waddle O,
  Jack sing saddle O,
  Blowsey boys bubble O,
  Under the broom.

I sold my cow, and I bought me a calf;
I'd fain have made a fortune, but lost the best
    half.
  With my wing, wang, waddle O,
  Jack sing saddle O,
  Blowsey boys bubble O,
  Under the broom.

I sold my calf, and I bought me a cat;
A pretty thing she was, in my chimney sat;
  With my wing, wang, waddle O,
  Jack sing saddle O,
  Blowsey boys bubble O,
  Under the broom.

I sold my cat, and bought me a mouse;
He carried fire in his tail, and burnt down my
      house;
  With my wing, wang, waddle O,
  Jack sing saddle O,
  Blowsey boys bubble O,
  Under the broom.

DANCE a baby diddy
  What can a mother do wid'e
But sit in a lap,
And give him some pap,
Dance a baby diddy.

O THAT I was where I would be,
  Then would I be where I am not.
But where I am I must be,
  And where I would be I cannot.

WE are all in the dumps,
　　For diamonds are trumps,
The kittens are gone to St. Paul's;
　　The babies are bit,
　　The moon's in a fit,
And the houses are built without walls.

ONE for the money,
　　Two for the show,
Three to make ready,
　　And four to go.

WHEN good King Arthur ruled his land,
　　He was a goodly king;
He bought three packs of barley meal,
　　To make a bag-pudding.

A bag-pudding the king did make,
　　And stuff'd it well with plums;
And in it put great lumps of fat,
　　As big as my two thumbs.

The king and queen did eat thereof,
　　And noblemen beside;
And what they could not eat that night,
　　The queen next morning fried.

I AM become of flesh and blood,
　　As other creatures be;
Yet there's neither flesh nor blood
　　Doth remain in me.
I make kings that they fall out;
　　I make them agree;
And yet there's neither flesh nor blood,
Doth remain in me.
　　　　　　　　[A Quill Pen.]

TOSS up my darling, toss him up high,
　　Don't let his head, though, hit the blue sky.

SEE Saw, Margery Daw,
The old hen flew over the malt house;
She counted her chickens one by one,
Still she missed the little white one,
And this is it, this is it, this is it.

THE winds they did blow,
The leaves they did wag;
Along came a beggar boy,
And put me in his bag—

He took me up to London,
A lady did me buy—
Put me in a silver cage
And hung me up on high—

With apples by the fire,
And nuts for to crack,
Besides a little feather-bed,
To rest my little back.

SIEVE my lady's oatmeal,
Grind my lady's flour;
Put it in a chestnut,
Let it stand an hour.

MARY had a pretty bird,—
Feathers bright and yellow;
Slender legs, upon my word,
He was a pretty fellow—
The sweetest notes he always sung,
Which much delighted Mary;
And near the cage she'd ever sit,
To hear her own canary.

AS round as an apple, as deep as a cup,
And all the king's horses can't pull it up.

[A Well.]

IF I had a mule, sir, and he wouldn't start,
Do you think I'd harness him up to a cart;
No, no. I'd give him oats and hay,
And let him stay there all the day.

THE lion and the unicorn
Were fighting for the crown;
The lion beat the unicorn
All round about the town.
Some gave them white bread,
And some gave them brown;
Some gave them plum-cake,
And sent them out of town.

APPLE-pie, pudding, and pancake,
All begins with A.

YANKEE Doodle went to town
Upon a little pony;
He stuck a feather in his hat,
And called it Macaroni.

A LITTLE pig found a fifty-dollar note,
And purchased a hat and a very fine coat,
With trousers, and stockings, and shoes;
Cravat, and shirt-collar, and gold-headed cane;
Then, proud as could be, did he march up the
lane;
Says he, "I shall hear all the news."

Mary, Mary, quite contrary, how does your garden grow?

(Page 130)

See-saw, Margery Daw, Jenny shall have a new mas

(Page

Curly locks! Curly locks! wilt thou be mine? Thou shalt not wash dishes, nor yet feed the swine.

Ring a-round a rosie, a pocket full of po.
(Page

COLD and raw the North winds blow,
  Bleak in the morning early,
All the hills are covered with snow,
  And winter's now come fairly.

LITTLE Tommy Tittlemouse,
  Lived in a little house;
He caught fishes
In other men's ditches.

OLD Mother Twitchett had but one eye,
  And a long tail, which she let fly;
And every time she went over a gap
She left a bit of her tail in a trap.
                [A Needle.]

JOHNNY Armstrong kill'd a calf,
  Peter Henderson got the half;
Willy Wilkinson got the head,—
Ring the bell, the calf is dead!

ONE-ERY, You-ery, E-kery, Haven,
  Hollow-bone, tallow-bone, ten or eleven.
Spin, Span, must be done,
Hollow-bone, tallow-bone, twenty-one.

DAME, get up and bake your pies,
  Bake your pies, bake your pies;
Dame, get up and bake your pies,
On Christmas-day in the morning.

Dame, what makes your maidens lie,
Maidens lie, maidens lie;
Dame, what makes your maidens lie,
On Christmas-day in the morning?

Dame, what makes your ducks to die,
Ducks to die, ducks to die;
Dame, what makes your ducks to die,
On Christmas day in the morning?

Their wings are cut and they cannot fly,
Cannot fly, cannot fly;
Their wings are cut and they cannot fly,
On Christmas-day in the morning.

RIDDLE me, riddle me, what is that
  Over the head, and under the hat?
                [Hair.]

TO market, to market, to buy a fat pig,
Home again, home again, jiggety jig.
To market, to market to buy a fat hog,
Home again, home again, jiggety jog.

AS I was going over Westminster Bridge,
I met with a Westminster scholar;
He pulled off his cap *an' drew* off his glove,
And wished me a very good morrow.
[What is his name.]

ONERY, ooery ickery Ann
Fillacy, follacy Nicholas John,
Quivy Quavy English navy,
Striggleum, Straggleum, buck!

LAVENDER blue and Rosemary green,
When I am king you shall be queen,
Call up my maids at four of the clock,
Some to the wheel and some to the rock,
Some to make hay, and some to thresh corn,
And you and I will keep the bed warm.

A DILLER, a dollar,
A ten o'clock scholar,
What makes you come so soon?
You used to come at ten o'clock,
But now you come at noon.

ROWLEY Powley, pudding and pie,
Kissed the girls and made them cry;
When the girls come out to play
Rowley Powley runs away.

THERE were two blind men went to see
Two cripples run a race;
The bull did fight the bumble-bee,
And scratched him in the face.

MY aunt she lost her petticoat,
My uncle found a calf,
My sister told an anecdote,
That made my father laugh.

A diller, a dollar, a ten o'clock scholar, What makes you come so soon?

WHAT shoemaker makes shoes without
        leather,
With all the four elements put together?
    Fire and water, earth and air;
    Ev'ry customer has two pair.
                [A Horseshoer.]

WHAT are little boys made of?
        Scizzors and snails,
And puppy dogs' tails,
And that's what little boys are
        made of.

What are little girls made of?
Sugar and spice,
And everything nice,
And that's what little girls are
        made of.

THERE was a man and he had naught,
        And robbers came to rob him;
He crept up to the chimney top,
    And then they thought they had him.

But he got down on t'other side,
    And then they could not find him;
He ran fourteen miles in fifteen days,
    And never look'd behind him.

"LITTLE maid, pretty maid, whither goest
        thou?"
"Down in the forest to milk my cow."
"Shall I go with thee?"   "No, not now;
When I send for thee, then come thou."

OLD King Cole was a merry old soul,
        And a merry old soul was he;
And he called for his pipe,
    And he called for his bowl,
And he called for his fiddlers three.
    And every fiddler, he had a fine fiddle,
And a very fine fiddle had he;
    "Tweedle dee, tweedle dee," said the fiddlers:
"Oh, there's none so rare as can compare
    With King Cole and his fiddlers three."

THE COURTSHIP AND MARRIAGE OF
COCK ROBIN AND JENNY WREN

IT was on a merry time,
   When Jenny Wren was young,
So neatly as she danced,
   And so sweetly as she sung,—

Robin Redbreast lost his heart:
   He was a gallant bird;
He doff'd his hat to Jenny,
   And thus to her he said:

" My dearest Jenny Wren,
   If you will but me mine,
You shall dine on cherry pie,
   And drink nice currant wine.

" I'll dress you like a Goldfinch
   Or like a Peacock gay;
So if you'll have me, Jenny,
   Let us appoint the day."

Jenny blush'd behind her fan,
   And thus declared her mind:
" Then let it be to-morrow, Bob,
   I take your offer kind;

" Cherry-pie is very good,
   So is currant wine;
But I'll wear my russet gown,
   And never dress to fine."

Robin rose up early,
   Before the break of day;
He flew to Jenny Wren's house,
   To sing a roundelay.

He met the Cock and Hen,
   And bade the Cock declare,
This was his wedding day,
   With Jenny Wren the fair.

The Cock then blew his horn,
   To let the neighbors know
This was Robin's wedding day,
   And they might see the show.

And first came Parson Rook,
   With his spectacles and band;
And one of Mother Hubbard's books
   He held within his hand.

The Sparrow and Tom-Tit,
  And many more, were there;
All came to see the wedding
  Of Jenny Wren, the fair.

Then follow'd him the Lark,
  For he could sweetly sing,
And he was to be the clerk
  At Cock Robin's wedding.

He sung of Robin's love
  For little Jenny Wren:
And when he came unto the end,
  Then he began again.

The Goldfinch came on next,
  To give away the bride;
The Linnet, being bridesmaid,
  Walk'd by Jenny's side;

And as she was a-walking,
  Said, "Upon my word,
I think that your Cock Robin
  Is a very pretty bird."

The Blackbird and the Thrush,
  And charming Nightingale,
Whose soft "jug" sweetly echoes
  Through every grove and dale

The Bullfinch walk'd by Robin,
  And thus to him did say:
"Pray mark, friend Robin Redbreast,
  That Goldfinch dress'd so gay;

What though her gay apparel
  Becomes her very well,
Yet Jenny's modest dress and look
  Must bear away the bell."

Then came the bride and bridegroom,
  Quite plainly was she dress'd,
And blush'd so much, her cheeks were
  As red as Robin's breast.

But Robin cheer'd her up,
  "My pretty Jen," said he,
"We're going to be married,
  And happy we shall be."

"Oh, then," says Parson Rook,
  "Who gives this maid away?"
"I do," says the Goldfinch,
  "And her fortune I will pay:

"Here's a bag of grain of many sorts,
  And other things beside:
Now happy be the bridegroom,
  And happy be the bride!"

"And will you have her, Robin,
  To be your wedded wife?"
"Yes, I will," says Robin,
  "And love her all my life!"

"And you will have him, Jenny,
  Your husband now to be?"
"Yes, I will," says Jenny,
  "And love him heartily!"

Then on her finger fair
  Cock Robin put the ring;
"You're married now," says Parson Rook,
  While the Lark aloud did sing:

" Happy be the bridegroom,
  And happy be the bride!
And may not man, nor bird, nor beast,
  This happy pair divide!"

The birds were ask'd to dine—
  Not Jenny's friends alone,
But every pretty songster
  That had Cock Robin known.

They had a cherry pie,
  Beside some currant wine,
And every guest brought something,
  That sumptuous they might dine.

Now they all sat or stood,
  To eat and to drink;
And every one said what
  He happen'd to think.

They each took a bumper,
  And drank to the pair,
Cock Robin the bridegroom,
  And Jenny the fair.

The dinner things removed,
  They all began to sing;
And soon they made the place
  Near a mile around to ring.

The concert it was fine,
  And every bird tried
Who best should sing for Robin,
  And Jenny Wren the bride.

When in came the Cuckoo,
  And made a great rout;
He caught hold of Jenny,
  And pull'd her about.

Cock Robin was angry,
  And so was the Sparrow,
Who fetch'd in a hurry
  His bow and his arrow.

His aim then he took,
  But he took it not right;
His skill was not good,
  Or he shot in a fright;

For the Cuckoo he miss'd,
  But Cock Robin he kill'd!
And all the birds morn'd
  That his blood was so spill'd.

THERE was a man, and his name was Dob,
  And he had a wife and her name was Mob,
And he had a dog, and he called it Cob,
And she had a cat, called Chitterabob.

THERE was a little nobby colt,
  His name was Nobby Gray;
His head was made of pouce straw,
  His tail was made of hay.
    He could ramble, he could trot,
    He could carry a mustard-pot,
    Round the town of Woodstock.
    Hey, Jenney, hey!

LONG legs, crocked thighs,
  Little head and no eyes.
            [Pair of Tongs.]

SHOE the wild horse, and shoe the gray mare;
  If the horse won't be shod, let him go bare.

AS I walked by myself,
  And talked to myself,
Myself said unto me,
Look to thyself, take care of thyself,
For nobody cares for thee.
I answered myself,
And said to myself
In the self-same repartee,
Look to thyself, or not look to thyself,
The self-same thing will be.

PRETTY John Watts,
  We are troubled with rats—
Will you drive them out of the house?
  We have mice, too, in plenty,
  That feast in the pantry;
But let them stay and nibble away—
What harm in a little brown mouse?

ROBIN-a-Bobbin
  Bent his bow,
Shot at a pigeon
  And killed a crow.

LITTLE lad, little lad,
    Where wast thou born?
Far off in Lancashire,
Under a thorn;
Where they sup sour milk
From a ram's horn.

GIVE my horse a ton of hay,
    And put him in the stable;
And do your best the live-long day,
    To make him comfortable.

WASH the dishes, wipe the dishes,
    Ring the bell for tea;
Three good wishes, three good kisses,
    I will give to thee.

GAME OF THE GIPSEY

[One child is selected for Gipsey, one for Mother, and one for Daughter Sue.   The Mother says:

I CHARGE my daughters, every one,
    To keep good house while I am gone.
You and you, (*points*) but specially *you*,
(*Or sometimes*, but specially Sue),
Or else I'll beat you black and blue.

During the Mother's absence the Gipsey comes in, entices a child away, and hides her.   This is repeated till all the children are hidden, when the Mother has to find them.

EGGS, butter, cheese, bread,
    Stick, stock, stone, dead.
Stick him up, stick him down,
Stick him in the old man's crown.

"WHAT do they call you?"
    "Patchy Dolly."
"Where were you born?"
"In the cow's horn."
"Where were you bred?"
"In the cow's head."
"Where will you die?"
"In the cow's eye."

IF a man who turnips cries
    Cries not when his father dies,
It is proof that he would rather
Have a turnip than his father.

A is Ann, with milk from the cow.

B is Benjamin, making a bow.

C is Charlotte, gathering flowers.

D is Dick, one of the mowers.

E is Eliza, feeding a hen.

F is Frank, mending his pen.

G is Georgiana, shooting an arrow.

H is Harry, wheeling a barrow.

I is Isabella, gathering fruit.

J is John, playing the flute.

K is Kate, nursing her dolly.

L is Lawrence, feeding poor Polly.

M is Maria, learning to draw.

N is Nicholas, with a jackdaw.

O is Octavius, riding a goat.

P is Penelope, sailing a boat.

Q is Quintus, armed with a lance.

R is Rachel, learning to dance.

S is Sarah, talking to cook.

T is Tommy, reading a book.

U is Urban, rolling the green.

V is Victoria, reading she's seen.

W is Walter, flying a kite.

X is Xerxes, a boy of great might.

Y is Miss Youthful, eating bread.

Z is Zachariah, going to bed.

LITTLE Betty Blue,
    Lost her holiday shoe.
What will poor Betty do?
Why, give her another,
To match the other,
And then she will walk in two.

THE old woman must stand at the tub, tub,
        tub,
The dirty clothes to rub, rub, rub;
But when they are clean, and fit to be seen,
She'll dress like a lady, and dance on the green.

JOSEPH Smith bought a rake,
    And sold it for some corn;
He lived a week on johnny cake,
    And now he's dead and gone.

COCK a doodle doo!
    My dame has lost her shoe;
My master's lost his fiddling stick,
And don't know what to do.

Cock a doodle doo!
What is my dame to do?
Till master finds his fiddling stick,
She'll dance without her shoe.

Cock a doodle doo!
My dame has lost her shoe,
And master's found his fiddling stick,
Sing, doodle, doodle, doo!

Cock a doodle doo!
My dame will dance with you,
While master fiddles his fiddling stick,
For dame and doodle doo.

Cock a doodle doo!
Dame has lost her shoe;
Gone to bed and scratch'd her head,
And can't tell what to do.

[The "Three Knights of Spain" is a game in which the children form themselves in two parties, one representing a courtly dame and her daughters, the other the suitors of the daughters. The last party, moving backwards and forwards, with their arms entwined, approach and recede from the mother party, which is stationary, singing to a very sweet air.]

SUITORS

WE are three brethren out of Spain,
 Come to court your daughter Jane.

MOTHER

My daughter Jane she is too young,
And has not learned her mother tongue.

SUITORS

Be she young, or be she old,
For her beauty she must be sold.
So fare you well, my lady gay,
We'll call again another day.

MOTHER

Turn back, turn back, thou scornful knight,
And rub thy spurs till they be bright.

SUITORS

Of my spurs take you no thought,
For in this town they were not bought—
So fare you well, my lady gay,
We'll call again another day.

MOTHER

Turn back, turn back, thou scornful knight,
And take the fairest in your sight.

SUITOR

The fairest maid that I can see
Is pretty Nancy,—come to me.

Here comes your daughter safe and sound,
Every pocket with a thousand pound;
Every finger with a gay gold ring;
Please to take your daughter in.

THATCHER of Thatchwood
 Went to Thatchet a-thatching;
Did a thatcher of Thatchwood go to
 Thatchet a-thatching?
If a thatcher of Thatchwood went to
 Thatchet a-thatching,
Where's the thatching the thatcher of
 Thatchwood has thatched—

"JACKY, come give me your fiddle,
 If you ever mean to thrive."
"Nay, I'll not give my fiddle
 To any man alive.
"If I should give my fiddle,
 They'll think that I'm gone mad,
For many a joyful day
 My fiddle and I have had."

ONCE in my life I married a wife,
  And where do you think I found her?
On Gretna Green in velvet sheen
  And I took up a stick to pound her—
She jumped over a barberry bush,
  And I jumped over a timber,
I showed her a gay gold ring
  And she showed me her finger.

A WATER there is, I must pass,
  A broader water never was;
And yet of all waters I ever did see,
  To pass over with less jeopardy.
      [The Dew.]

LITTLE drops of water,
  Little grains of sand,
Make the mighty ocean,
  And the pleasant land.

CACKLE, cackle, Madam Goose!
  Have you any feathers loose?
Truly have I, little fellow,
Half enough to fill a pillow;
And here are quills, take one or ten,
And make from each, pop-gun or pen.

THE greedy man is he who sits
  And bites bits out of plates,
Or else takes up an almanac
  And gobbles all the dates.

AT the siege of Belleisle,
  I was there all the while,
All the while, all the while,
At the siege of Belleisle.

ON Saturday night, it shall be my care
  To powder my locks and curl my hair.
On Sunday morning, my love will come in,
When he will marry me with a gold ring.

HICKORY, dickory, sackory down!
  How many miles to Richmond town?
Turn to the left and turn to the right,
And you may get there by Saturday night.

I HAD a little moppet,
I kept it in my pocket
  And fed it with corn and hay—
There came a proud beggar,
  Who swore he would have her,
And stole my moppet away.

AN apple pie, when it looks nice,
  Would make one long to have a slice,
But if the taste should prove so, too,
I fear one slice would scarcely do.
So to prevent my asking twice,
Pray, Mamma, cut a good large slice.

HUSH thee, my babby,
    Lie still with thy daddy,
Thy mammy has gone to the mill
    To grind thee some wheat,
    To make thee some meat,
And so my dear babby lie still.

THERE was an old woman sat spinning,
  And that the first beginning;
      She had a calf,
      And that's half;
      She took it by the tail,
And threw it over the wall,
And that's all!

TOMMY'S tears, and Mary's fears
Will make them old before their years.

1. I am a gold lock.
2. I am a gold key.
1. I am a silver lock.
2. I am a silver key.
1. I am a brass lock.
2. I am a brass key.
1. I am a lead lock.
2. I am a lead key.
1. I am a monk lock.
2. I am a monk key.

MOSS was a little man, and a little mare
    did buy;
For kicking and for sprawling, none her could
    come nigh;
She could trot, she could amble, and could
    canter here and there,
But one night she strayed away—so Moss lost
    his mare.

Moss got up next morning to catch her fast
    asleep,
And round about the frosty fields so nimbly he
    did creep,
Dead in a ditch he found her, and glad to find
    her there;
So I'll tell you by-and-by how Moss caught
    his mare.

"Rise! stupid, rise!" he thus to her did say;
"Arise, you beast, you drowsy beast, get up
    without delay,
For I must ride you to the town, so don't lie
    sleeping there;
He put the halter round her neck so Moss
    caught his mare.

MARCH winds and April showers
    Bring forth May flowers.

RIDE a cock-horse to Shrewsbury cross,
    To buy little Johnny a galloping horse:
It trots behind and it ambles before,
And Johnny shall ride—till he can ride no more.

LITTLE Poll Parrot
    Sat in her garret,
Eating toast and tea;
    A little brown mouse
    Jumped into the house,
And stole it all away.

DANCE, Thumbkin, dance;
        (keep the thumb in motion
Dance, ye merrymen, everyone;
        (all the fingers in motion
For Thumbkin, he can dance alone;
        (the thumb alone moving
Thumbkin, he can dance alone;
        (the thumb alone moving
Dance, Foreman, dance,
        (the first finger moving
Dance, ye merrymen, everyone;
        (all moving
But Foreman he can dance alone,
        (the first finger moving
Foreman, he can dance alone,
        (the first finger moving
Dance, Longman, dance,
        (the second finger moving
Dance, ye merrymen, everyone;
        (all moving
For Longman he can dance alone,
        (the second finger moving
Longman, he can dance alone.
        (the second finger moving
Dance, Ringman, dance,
        (the third finger moving

Dance, ye merrymen, dance;
        (all moving
But Ringman cannot dance alone,
        (the third finger moving
Ringman, he cannot dance alone.
        (the third finger moving
Dance, Littleman, dance,
        (the fourth finger moving
Dance, ye merrymen, dance,
        (all moving
But Littleman, he can dance alone,
        (the fourth finger moving
Littleman, he can dance alone.
        (the fourth finger moving

THERE were three jovial Welchmen,
    As I have heard them say,
And they would go a-hunting
    Upon St. David's day.

All the day they hunted,
    And nothing could they find,
But a ship a-sailing,
    A-sailing with the wind.

One said it was a ship,
    The other he said, Nay;
The third said it was a house,
    With the chimney blown away.

And all the night they hunted,
    And nothing could they find
But the moon a-gliding,
    A-gliding with the wind.

One said it was the moon,
    The other he said, Nay;
The third said it was a cheese,
    An half o't cut away.

And all the day they hunted,
    And nothing could they find
But a hedgehog in a bramble-bush,
    And that they left behind.

The first said it was a hedgehog,
    The second he said, Nay;
The third said it was a pin-cushion,
    And the pins stuck in wrong way.

And all the night they hunted,
    And nothing could they find
But a hare in a turnip-field
    And that they left behind.

The first said it was a hare,
    The second he said, Nay;
The third said it was a calf,
    And the cow had run away.

And all the day they hunted,
    And nothing could they find
But an owl in a holly-tree,
    And that they left behind.

One said it was an owl,
    The other he said, Nay;
The third said 'twas an old man,
    And his beard growing grey.

THERE was an old crow
    Sat upon a clod;
There's an end of my song
    That's odd!

THERE was a monkey climb'd up a tree,
  When he fell down, then down fell he.

There was a crow sat on a stone,
When he was gone, then there was none.

There was an old wife did eat an apple,
When she had ate two, she had ate a couple.

There was a horse going to the mill,
When he went on, he stood not still.

There was a butcher cut his thumb,
When it did bleed, then blood did come.

There was a lackey ran a race,
When he ran fast, he ran apace.

There was a cobbler clowting shoon,
When they were mended, they were done.

There was a chandler making candle,
When he them strip, he did them handle.

There was a navy went into Spain,
When it return'd, it came again.

A NICK and a nock
  A hen and a cock
And a penny for my master.

MARGARET wrote a letter,
  Sealed it with her finger,
Threw it in the dam
  For the dusty miller.

Dusty was his coat,
  Dusty was the siller,
Dusty was the kiss
  I'd from the dusty miller.

If I had my pockets
  Full of gold and siller,
I would give it all
  To *my dusty miller*.

A LITTLE old man of Derby,
  How do you think he served me?
He took away my bread and cheese,
And that is how he served me.

LITTLE Robin Redbreast sat upon a tree—
  Up went the Pussy-cat, and down went he:
Down came Pussy-cat, away Robin ran—
Says little Robin Redbreast—catch me if you can.

Little Robin Redbreast jumped upon a wall,
Pussy-cat jumped after him, and got a little fall.
Little Robin chirped and sung, and what did Pussy say?
Pussy-cat said mew, mew, mew—and Robin flew away.

CURLY locks! Curly locks! wilt thou be mine?
Thou shalt not wash dishes, nor yet feed the swine;
But sit on a cushion and sew a fine seam,
And feed upon strawberries, sugar and cream!

WHO ever saw a rabbit
  Dressed in a riding-habit,
Gallop off to see her friends, in this style?
  I should not be surprised
  If my lady is capsized,
  Before she has ridden half a mile.

THERE was a little man,
  And he had a little gun,
And his bullets were made of lead, lead, lead;
  He went to the brook
  And saw a little duck,
And he shot it through the head, head, head.

  He carried it home
  To his old wife Joan,
And bid a fire for to make, make, make,
  To roast the little duck,
  He had shot in the brook,
And he'd go and fetch her the drake, drake, drake.

AS I was going o'er London Bridge,
  I met a cart full of fingers and thumbs!
[Gloves.]

AS I was going up the hill,
  I met with Jack the piper,
And all the tune that he could play
  Was, "Tie up your petticoats tighter."

I tied them once, I tied them twice,
  I tied them three times over;
And all the song that he could sing
  Was, "Carry me safe to Dover."

SIMPLE Simon met a pieman
   Going to the fair;
Says Simple Simon to the pieman,
   "Let me taste your ware."

Says the pieman to Simple Simon,
   "Show me first your penny."
Says Simple Simon to the pieman,
   "Indeed I have not any."

Simple Simon went a-hunting,
   For to catch a hare,
He rode an ass about the streets,
   But couldn't find one there.

He went to shoot a wild duck,
   But wild duck flew away;
Says Simon, I can't hit him,
   Because he will not stay.

He went for to eat honey
   Out of the mustard-pot,
He bit his tongue until he cried—
   That was all the good he got.

He went to ride a spotted cow,
   That had a little calf,
She threw him down upon the ground,
   Which made the people laugh.

Simple Simon went a-fishing
   For to catch a whale;
All the water he had got
   Was in his mother's pail.

Once Simon made a great snow-ball,
   And brought it in to roast;
He laid it down before the fire,
   And soon the ball was lost.

He went to catch a dickey-bird,
   And thought he could not fail,
Because he'd got a little salt
   To put upon his tail.

Simple Simon went to look
   If plums grew on a thistle;
He pricked his fingers very much,
   Which made poor Simon whistle.

He went for water in a sieve,
   But soon it all run through,
And now poor Simple Simon
   Bids you all adieu.

RING the bell!
   Knock at the door!
Lift up the latch!
And walk in!

WHISTLE, daughter, whistle; whistle,
    daughter dear.
I cannot whistle, mammy, I cannot whistle clear.
Whistle, daughter, whistle, whistle for a pound.
I cannot whistle, mammy, I cannot make a
    sound.

THERE was an old man who lived in a
    wood,
  As you may plainly see;
He said he could do as much work in a day,
  As his wife could do in three.

"With all my heart," the old woman said;
  "If that you will allow,
To-morrow you'll stay at home in my stead,
  And I'll go drive the plough;

"But you must milk the Tidy cow,
  For fear that she go dry;
And you must feed the little pigs
  That are within the sty;

"And you must mind the speckled hen,
  For fear she lay astray;
And you must reel the spool of yarn
  That I spun yesterday."

The old woman took a staff in her hand,
  And went to drive the plough;
The old man took a pail in his hand,
  And went to milk the cow;

But Tidy hinched, and Tidy flinched,
  And Tidy broke his nose,
And Tidy gave him such a blow,
  That the blood ran down to his toes.

"Hi! Tidy! ho! Tidy! hi!
  Tidy, do stand still!
If ever I milk you, Tidy, again,
  'Twill be sore against my will."

He went to feed the little pigs,
  That were within the sty;
He hit his head against the beam,
  And he made the blood to fly.

He went to mind the speckled hen,
  For fear she'd lay astray,
And he forgot the spool of yarn
  His wife spun yesterday.

So he swore by the sun, the moon, and the stars,
  And the green leaves on the tree,
If his wife didn't do a day's work in her life,
  She should ne'er be ruled by he.

JOCKETY jog—jockety jog,
  Over the hills, and over the bog.

Jockety jog—jockety jog,
Many a mile this day I've trod.

Jockety jog—jockety jog,
I'm the Milkman's horse, old Naggetty Nogg.

Jockety jog—jockety jog,
My Master's name is Reuney K. Rogg.

Jockety jog—jockety jog,
He's a good man—he drinks no grog.

Jockety jog—jockety jog,
Never does he old Naggetty flog.

Jockety jog—jockety jog,
I'll bear him safe through all this fog.

Jockety jog—jockety jog,
How the darkness the way doth clog.

Jockety jog—jockety jog,
I'm not afraid of the bark of a dog.

Jockety jog— jockety jog,
I'm not afraid of the croak of a frog.

Jockety jog—jockety jog,
I know a toad from a polliwog.

Jockety jog—jockety jog,
I'm not afraid of the grunt of a hog.

Jockety jog—jockety jog,
I'll not stumble over that log.

Jockety jog—jockety jog,
Over the hills, and over the bog.

Jockety jog—jockety jog,
Safe home through all the fog.

Jockety jog—jockety jog,
Safe home—Reuney K. Rogg.

Jockety jog—jockety jog,
Safe home—old Naggetty Nog.

LITTLE King Boggen he built a fine hall,
  Pie-crust and pastry-crust, that was the
    wall,
The windows were made of black puddings
    and white,
And slated with pancakes,—you ne'er saw the
    like.

I'VE seen you where you never were,
    And where you ne'er will be,
And yet you in that very same place
May still be seen by me.
    [Your Reflection in a Mirror.]

WASN'T it funny? hear it all people!
    Little Tom Thum has swallowed a steeple!
How did he do it?
I'll tell you, my son:
'Twas made of white sugar—and easily done!

MADE in London,
        Sold at New York,
Stops a bottle,
    And is a cork.

WHEN I was taken from the fair body,
    They then cut off my head,
And thus my shape was altered.
It's I that make peace between King and ring,
And many a true lover glad.
All this I do, and ten times more,
And more I could do still;
But nothing can I do
Without my guider's will.
        [A quill pen.]

WHEN little Fred went to bed,
    He always said his prayers;
He kissed mamma, and then papa,
    And straightway went up-stairs.

RING-a-ring-a roses,
    A pocket full of posies;
Hush—hush—hush—
We'll all tumble down.

THERE was an old woman
  And nothing she had;
And so this old woman
  Was said to be mad.
She'd nothing to eat,
  She'd nothing to wear,
She'd nothing to lose,
  She'd nothing to fear,
She'd nothing to ask,
  And nothing to give,
And when she did die,
  She'd nothing to leave.

CANTALOUPES! Cantaloupes! What is
  the price?
Eight for a dollar, and all very nice.

DING, dong, bell,
  Pussy's in the well!
Who put her in?
Little Johnny Green;
Who pulled her out,
Big Tom Stout;
What a naughty boy was that
To try and drown poor pussy cat,
Who never did any harm,
And killed the mice in his father's barn.

POLLY, Dolly, Kate and Molly,
  All are filled with pride and folly.
Polly tattles, Dolly wriggles,
Katy rattles, Molly giggles;
Whoe'er knew such constant rattling,
Wriggling, giggling, noise, and tattling.

AT reck'ning let's play,
    and prithee, let's lay
A wager, and let it be this:
    Who first to the sum
Of twenty doth come,
Shall have for his winning a kiss.

I SING, I sing,
    From morn till night,
From cares I'm free, and my heart is light.

PINCHING, plodding Peter Clide
    Never gave a cent!
His only sorrow when he died
    Was for a dollar lent.

Pinching, plodding Peter Clide
    Labored hard for money;
When he got it, then he died
    And left it all to Sonny.

AT early morn the spiders spin,
    And by and by the flies drop in;
And when they call the spiders say,
Take off your things and stay all day.

RUMSEY Dumsey's come to town
    On a speckled pony;
He wears a hat without a crown,
    And says he has no money.

COME to the window,
    My baby, with me,
And look at the stars
    That shine on the sea!
There are two little stars
    That play at bo-peep
With two little fish
    Far down in the deep;
And two little frogs
    Cry neap, neap, neap;
I see a dear baby
    That should be asleep.

OLD Toby Sizer is such a miser,
    No cloak he'll buy to keep him dry, sir.
He'll not permit his neighbor, Randal,
To light his pipe by his short candle,
For fear, he says, he might convey
A little bit of light away.

GAY go up, and gay go down,
To ring the bells of London town.

Bulls' eyes and targets,
Say the bells of St. Marg'ret's.

Brickbats and tiles,
Say the bells of St. Giles'.

Halfpence and farthings,
Say the bells of St. Martin's.

Oranges and lemons,
Say the bells of St. Clement's.

Pancakes and fritters,
Say the bells of St. Peter's.

Two sticks and an apple,
Say the bells at Whitechapel.

Old Father Baldpate,
Say the slow bells at Aldgate.

Pokers and tongs,
Say the bells at St. John's.

Kettles and pans,
Say the bells at St. Ann's.

You owe me ten shillings,
Say the bells at St. Helen's.

When will you pay me?
Say the bells at Old Bailey.

When I grow rich,
Say the bells at Shoreditch.

Pray, when will that be?
Say the bells of Stepney.

I am sure I don't know,
Says the great bell at Bow.

Here comes a candle to light you to bed,
And here comes a chopper to chop off your head.

F for a fig,

I for a jig, and

N for knuckle-bones,

I for John the waterman, and

S for sack of stones.